LESSONS FROM HISTORY
A Celebration in Blackness

Jr.-Sr. High Edition

by Jawanza Kunjufu

Illustrated by Yaounde Olu and Cornell Barnes

African American Images
Chicago, Illinois

i

Photo Credits
Argonne Laboratory
Final Call
NASA
Vivian Harsh Collection
William Hall

Cover Illustration by Yaounde Olu

First Edition
Seventh Printing

Dedication

To Mrs. Avery, Hudson, Allen, Butler, Foote, Marks, Mr. Payne, Boughton, and Richards, all Black teachers who taught me Black history by being positive role models, who demanded excellence.

To African-American children who deserve more than Negro history, which gives them only one day of lessons about Africa, two days of lessons on the slaveship, and the remainder of the course being slavery or fighting racism in America, Negro history — all taught in February, the shortest month of the year.

To Carol Finn, who just happens to be a White principal of African-American children, who inspired me to write this textbook. I had planned to write *Lessons from History* in 1988 as a story book. She reminded me that there is no comprehensive Black history textbook in print for the elementary and junior high school student.

Special Thanks

Special thanks is given to Kawana Sherman, Janice Crayton, Yolanda Taylor, and Mary Brown for their editorial assistance. A special thanks is given to Sanyika Anwisye who spent long hours with me editing and rewriting the manuscript, lastly, my family that went without a husband and father many days, but encouraged me to continue.

Preface

In this book Black people will be called Africans or African-Americans. Why? Because Black people wherever they are, come from the *land* called Africa. We have been called by many different names — colored, Negro, Black, etc. Most people are known by the land which they or their ancestors lived in or come from. Germans are called Germans because there is a land named Germany. Irish are called Irish because there is a land named Ireland. Chinese are called Chinese because there is a land called China. Mexicans are called Mexicans because there is a land named Mexico. Now look at the map. Is there a place called Colorland? Negroland? Blackland? No. There is a land named Africa, which is where we came from. So, in our book, we shall refer to ourselves as Africans, African-Americans, and Africans in America.

Table of Contents

Chapter One

Africa, The Beginning of Civilization

Africa is the second largest continent in the world with an area of twelve million square miles.

Most maps show the United States and Africa as equal in size, but Africa is almost three times as large.

Often people think of Africa as a country. Africa is composed of 54 different countries covering its entire area.

The longest river in the world, the Nile, along with the Niger and Congo rivers provide Africa with much of its water. One of the tallest mountains in the world, Mount Kilimanjaro, rises nearly twenty thousand feet to its snow-capped peak, Kibo, in the East African nation of Tanzania. Africa is mostly tropical as it stretches from 37° north latitude to 35° south latitude. Africa has a large desert region known as the Sahara.

Humans have always wanted to know their roots. The story of Adam and Eve is an expression of this desire. The study of anthropology and the search for buried fossils are attempts to measure the age, location, race and other characteristics of human existence. Originally it was estimated that man is two million years old and his birthplace was Africa. The research has continued through scientists Richard Leakey, Donald Johnson, J. Desmond Clark and others. Current estimates suggest that humans are over four million years old. The Chinese or Peking Java man is predicted to be 700 thousand years old and the European or Neanderthal man is assumed to be 70 thousand years old.

The birthplace of humanity is in Africa. People born close to the equator have darker pigment and possess more melanin both in their skin and eyes. When Africans traveled to Asia and Europe, they saw lighter skinned people, with longer hair and narrow facial features. In colder climates, one receives less sun; because it's colder one needs more hair to cover the head, and a narrower nose to absorb less frigid air. Race is not a biological term; it's scientifically inaccurate to place five billion people into three groups—negroid, mongoloid, and caucasoid. Humans vary with the climate. To repeat: the birthplace of the human race — all of it — is in Africa. Race is a sociological term used by humans to categorize.

The oldest and one of the most noted statues is the Sphinx of Gizeh. The combination of man and beast, brain and body was worshipped as God. There have been many pyramids built in Egypt. Imhotep was the chief architect for the first stone pyramid, called the Step Pyramid, in 2780 B.C. The pyramids of Gizeh are the largest. One of these, named after Pharaoh Khufu (called Cheops in Greek) is 48 stories high, 755 feet wide, and was made with 2,300,000 stones, each weighing three tons. It took sixty years to finish and both the Sphinx and Khufu's pyramid are considered two of the seven wonders of the world. They are the only two remaining.

Napoleon was so jealous of this great feat he ordered twenty-one shells of fire aimed at the face of the Sphinx to alter its facial features so people would not know it was African. Despite the damage from this "twenty-one gun salute," the Sphinx is still recognizably African. It has been rumored that the Jews built the pyramids as slaves; but the Jews, led by Abraham, did not arrive until 1640 B.C. This was twelve hundred years after the pyramids of Gizeh were constructed. Africans also built large temples, tombs, and obelisks that still stand. Much of the architecture designed by Africans 5,000 years ago is still being imitated today. The Eiffel Tower in Paris, Big Ben Tower in London, and the

3

Washington Monument in Washington, D.C. are shining examples of flattery to Egypt. Africans developed the laws of mathematics and science. They were the first to provide a written language, which is called hieroglyphics. Some people call the period before Christ, "prehistory" because they did not know how to write. Africans call it "history" because they could.

Imhotep was the father of medicine. Many history books say that Hippocrates was the first doctor. Imhotep lived in the era of 2800 B.C., but Hippocrates was not born until 2000 years later. The Greek name for Imhotep is Aesculapius. Doctors today still take this oath, in which Hippocrates refers to Imhotep:

"I swear by Apollo the physician, and Aesculapius, and Health, and all-heal, and all the gods and goddesses, that according to my ability and judgment, I will keep this oath and this stipulation to reckon him who taught me this art equally dear to me as my parents, to share my substance with him, and relieve his necessities if required;...."

Africans founded the first university, the Grand Lodge of Wa'at. The Greeks renamed it the Grand Lodge of Thebes, and the Arabs have changed it to the City of Luxor. The Greeks studied under the Egyptians. The professors were priests. The curriculum was called the mystery system and was divided into four areas: religion, liberal arts, applied sciences, and business. Most students entered at the age of seven and did not complete their studies until forty years later.

The introduction of the lunar and solar calendars and the study of astronomy were made by Africans. Dr. Alfred Wallace, speaking before the British Association the Advance of Science in 1876, concluded: "That the pyramid of Gizeh is truly square, the sides being equal and the angles right angles; that the four sockets on level; that the directions of the sides are accurately the four cardinal points; that the vertical height of the pyramid bears the same proportion to its circumference at the base as the radius of a circle does to its circumference. Now all of these measures, angles, and levels are accurate, not as an ordinary surveyor or builder could make them, but to such a degree as requires the best *Modern Instruments.*"

The above is mentioned so the world can see that Pythagoras did not create the theorem. The Egyptian philosophy "man know thyself," did not come from Thales, Plato, and Socrates, but is inscribed on the walls at the Grand Lodge of Wa'at where they

4

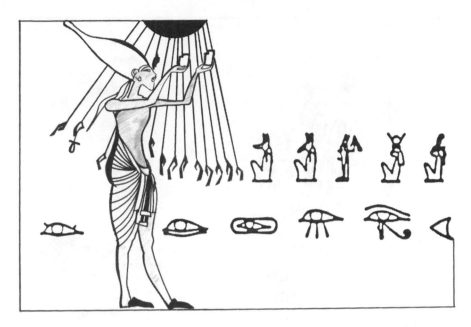

studied. Herodotus is not the father of history, because history was being recorded inside the tombs, temples, pyramids, and on papyrus (original paper) 3,000 years before his birth. The greatest insult of all, and the reason why George James called his book *Stolen Legacy* came about when Greek King Alexander invaded Egypt, and Aristotle stole the books. Aristotle is thus falsely credited with writing over 1000 books on a wide range of subjects — books which were written by Africans.

Africans had great kings and queens. Some of the kings were Akhenaten also called Amen-ho-tep, Tutankhamon, and Ramses II. Some of the queens were N'Zinga, Hatshepsut, and Nefertiti. More will be said about Ramses II and Queen N'Zinga in Chapter Four on military heroes and heroines. Queen Hatshepsut was also a Pharaoh and sometimes dressed in royal male attire. Queen Hatshepsut was a brilliant leader. She worked with her council of elders, and expanded foreign trade, brought peace between southern and northern Egypt, and undertook one of the largest building programs in history.

Queen Nefertiti was the mother-in-law of King Tutankhamon, and wife of King Akhenaten. Nefertiti, which means, "beautiful one is here," had a great influence on her husband. She was actively involved in religious and artistic development.

The beginning of religion was in Africa. Pharaoh Akhenaten or Amen-hotep gave the world the belief in one God. The ankh is the sign of life. The cross is shaped almost like the ankh. The word ankh is a part of the Pharaoh's name. Africans believed in one God, Amon-Ra, which represented the sun. Amon is very close to Amen, which is how Christians end their prayers, and Amin, which is how Muslims end their prayers.

The ancients viewed the sacred image of God as Black. The Gods of Antiquity from Egypt to India are: Osiris of Egypt, Zeus of Greece, Apollo of Greece, Isis of Rome, Horus of Rome, Fulti of China, Zaha of Japan, and Krishna of India.

The Shrine of the Black Madonna is still viewed in Spain, Russia, and Poland—especially by Pope John Paul II. It was only during the European Renaissance that Michaelangelo was commissioned to paint Jesus White.

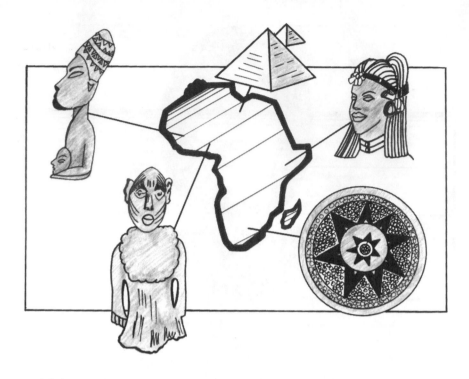

Africans lived all over the continent. Great empires were built in Ethiopia and Nubia, now called the Sudan. The world's oldest iron smelting mine was in Swaziland in the southern area of Africa. Great communities included the Masai, Yoruba, Zulu, Nubian, and Ashanti.

While much credit is given to Egypt and the Grand Lodge of Wa'at, other great empires included Ghana, Mali, and Songhay. The increasing onslaught of the Sahara forced Africans to migrate westward. Ghana was known as "Land of the Gold." They too were involved in iron mining and farming. At their height in 1000 A.D., King Tenhamenin could field 200,000 warriors in battle. Mali eventually overtook Ghana in 1200 A.D. Under the leadership of Sunni Ali, Songhay became a power in the fifteenth century. It was in Songhay in the city of Timbuktu, that the great University of Sankore was founded. All three of these empires were victims of the desert, complacency, and internal strife.

Unfortunately, the history of the world is full of countries conquering each other to acquire power. The reign of most empires is relatively short within the context of human history.

Africans were great travelers and master shipbuilders. They had sailed to America over 3,000 years before Columbus. Carlos Marquez, the Mexican explorer, observed skeletons of Africans from Bolivia to Mexico. The Olmec civilization left sculptural evidence showing African features. The numerous pyramids in Mexico have the same north-south axis as the Eqyptian pyramids.

Africans from Morocco, called Moors, traveled to Europe and ruled Spain from 711 to 1400 A.D. under General Tarik. He was such a strong leader that the Rock of Gibraltar, also a symbol of strength, was associated with Tarik. Playwright William Shakespeare was so inspired by the Moors that he wrote a play about one. The play, *Othello,* showcased Black male strength. The Moors brought lighted streets, public baths, map skills, and a globe to the Spaniards who thought at that time the world was flat.

Africa has many natural resources including the largest supply of gold and diamonds in the world. Africa possesses abundant supplies of many of the minerals needed to run industries. Some of these are cobalt, uranium, copper, aluminum, and bauxite. The tropical climate produced an abundance of food. The expanding desert and lack of crop rotation is causing the present food shortage. The climatic and personality differences between Africa and Europe led the famous historian, Cheikh Anta Diop, to propose

the "Two Cradle Theory." It stated that Africa, the southern "cradle," was warm and had an abundance of food; therefore, it became settled and farmed. Because less time and energy were needed to secure food, Africans had time and energy to build pyramids and universities. Europe in the northern "cradle," with its cold climate where nature was an enemy and food had to be hunted, created a nomadic life-style.

Modern Africa is very different from what we see on television. Mass media portrays Africa as primitive and Tarzan as conqueror. Africa has large cities, hotels, office buildings, and cars. It also has country farms, roads, and animals. There are about 500 million people in Africa.

Bibliography

Adult

Carruthers, Jacob. *Essays in Ancient Egyptian Studies.* Los Angeles: University of Sankore Press, 1984.

Diop, Cheikh Anta. *The African Origin of Civilization.* New York: Lawrence Hill, 1974.

_____. *The Cultural Unity of Black Africa.* Chicago: Third World Press, 1978.

Hilliard, Asa. *From Ancient Africa to African-Americans Today.* Portland: Portland Public Schools, 1983.

Jackson, John. *Man, God and Civilization.* Secaucus: Citadel Press, 1972.

James, George. *Stolen Legacy.* San Francisco: Julian Richardson, 1976.

Jochannon, Yosef Ben. *African Origins of the Major Western Religions.* New York: Alkebu-lan, 1970.

_____. *Black Man of the Nile.* New York: Alkebu-lan, 1981.

Kush, Indus Khamit. *What They Never Told You in History Class.* New York: Luxorr Publications, 1983.

Sertima, Ivan Van. *They Came Before Columbus.* New York: Random House, 1976.

Williams, Chancellor. *Destruction of Black Civilization.* Chicago: Third World Press, 1974.

Vocabulary

Write the definition for each word. Write a sentence using each word. Draw a picture of your favorite word on the list or in the chapter.

Anthropology
Architect
Astronomy
Attire
Axis
Bauxite
Civilization
Climate
Commission
Continent
Curriculum
Equator

Foreign
Fossils
Latitude
Lunar
Monument
Oath
Pigment
Sculpture
Solar
Tropical
University

Questions

1. Where was the original man born?
2. Describe the pyramid of Gizeh.
3. Who was Imhotep?
4. List the Greeks who some books credit with being first in medicine, math, history, and philosophy.
5. List two African queens and their accomplishments.
6. Describe the origins of religion.
7. Did Columbus discover America? Describe the Olmec civilization.
8. What is the "Two Cradle Theory"?

Exercises

1. With clay design a sphinx.
2. Draw a picture of King Akhenaten and Queen Nefertiti.
3. View a contemporary movie on Africa that shows the great pyramids, temples, tombs, empires, universities, and its abundant resources and modern facilities — avoid Tarzan movies, unless you show all its contradictions, including the relationship between Tarzan, Superman, and White male supremacy.

Chapter Two

The Invaders

There were many invaders of Africa. They included Asians, Arabs, Greeks, Romans, and northern Europeans. Africans welcomed them to their land. They provided them with food, water, tours, and traded goods. Africans treated them as visitors, friends, and business partners.

Asians and Arabs settled along the strategic north coast. They enjoyed the "Bread Basket of the World," the Nile valley. The longest river in the world, the Nile, flows northward and empties out in this northern region. Unfortunately, it took valuable minerals from the land in its 4,127 mile journey, leaving other countries very poor. As more visitors, friends, and business partners occupied the rich coastal region, Africans were forced to live in the poorer interior.

Asians, Arabs, and Europeans had come from places that were cold and with few resources. They enjoyed the warm air, fruit on the vines, and gold in the mines. They also saw how nice Africans treated them. This reinforces Diop's two cradle theory of climate and personality—a colder climate can make a person competitive and selfish, while a warm climate is conducive for producing cooperation and sharing. The invaders decided to take the land and make Africans slaves.

In the previous chapter, we discussed the tremendous advancement that Africans made in math and science. Iron was abundant in Africa and the world's oldest smelting mine was in Swaziland. They produced carbon steel in preheated furnaces with higher temperatures than European machines achieved until modern times.

Africans used their technology for constructive purposes and built pyramids, temples, tombs, and universities. Their tools of war were primitive, consisting primarily of spears, shields, and knives. The invaders had swords, knives, arrows, and eventually guns. This situation continues today in South Africa and with the world's nuclear arms race. The Africans' lack of self-defense was poor judgment.

The invaders saw a large rich land, with Africans divided into 1,000 communities, speaking over 2,000 languages. They saw a people naive enough to allow them to occupy the coast. This area is strategic because whoever controls it determines who enters and exits the continent. Africans allowed the invaders to live on the coast, which eventually reduced their trading, and forced them into the interior where the Nile was not as generous to the soil.

Slavery has existed all over the world, and Africa is no exception. There were African slaves who helped build the pyramids. When the invaders arrived, they observed slavery. Slavery also existed in Asia and Europe. The African value system had a different meaning for slavery and war. Often African communities would engage in war, but the outcome was surrender, not death for the defeated group. For example, the Masai would sur-

round the Gikuyu, establishing victory and then they would let the Gikuyu escape.

This same value system applied to slavery. A person could be a slave, but not suffer the extremes of psychological and physical brutality that were the norm in American slavery. African slavery did not include lynching, selling family members to different locations; nor was it a permanent existence for its slaves. This form of slavery was similar to what Europeans called indentured servitude. This structure allowed servants to buy their freedom, and have certain rights surrounding their lives.

African kings, pharaohs, and leaders assumed the invaders were operating under the same value system of slavery. Some African leaders were trying to protect their community from the invaders and were forced to buy weapons for slaves. The invaders did not sell them the best weapons, those were reserved for them. There were other African leaders who were greedy and sold slaves not for community protection, but for profit, and rum. The Middle Passage or triangle includes West Africa, the southeastern region of North America, and the islands of the West Indies. Ships would take sugar and molasses from the islands to North America for rum and guns, which were sold to kings in Africa for slaves, who were taken to the islands and America.

Africans were taken to the western coast to await the slave ships. This region includes the present countries of Gambia, Senegal, Liberia, Sierra Leone, Guinea, Ivory Coast, Ghana, Togo, Dahomey, and Nigeria. The invaders built slave forts at York, Atim, Cape Coast, Bena, and Goree Island.

16

The Africans were farmers, herders, traders, teachers, and priests. While they waited for the unknown, they thought about this maybe being the last time they would see their homeland.

The wait seemed forever and the chains were so tight, they caused bleeding even if the slave sat still. African people and the invaders continued fighting. Often the invaders would make the slaves fight on their side in exchange for rum, guns, or freedom. The Asian invasions began 6,000 years ago or 4,000 B.C. The Arab slave trade began around 2040 B.C., and Europe and America started in the fifteenth century and proceeded through the nineteenth century.

When the slave ships arrived, Africans were placed on them like animals and packed as closely as sardines. They were forced to lie chained next to each other. There was no room to move legs or arms. Most ships had a capacity of 200, but sailed with over 700 slaves. The trip to the West Indies or America lasted about two months.

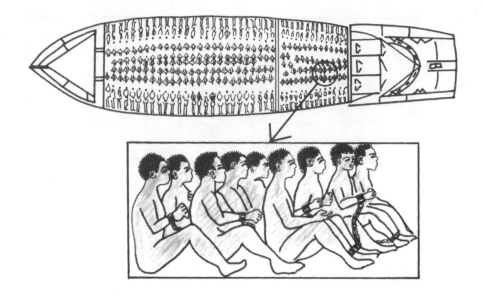

Slaves had a difficult decision: to accept slavery and possibly live; or, to rebel thereby risking death; or, to commit suicide rather than be enslaved. No person wants to be a slave and very few sane people voluntarily commit suicide. Africans pondered the choices between overthrowing the ship or jumping off. Very few, if any, Africans willingly accepted their current fate. For many, being a slave was unacceptable; they did not eat or drink in hopes of starvation, some killed their babies, poisoned themselves, or jumped off the ship to the awaiting sharks who followed slave ships. (In fact, sharks followed slave ships for just that reason — to attack slaves who jumped or were thrown overboard.) They refused to be slaves and profit their owners. They believed in life after death and hoped their spirits would return to Africa.

For others, rebellion and revolt seemed a more viable option. Often the owners would let the women and children walk freely along the upper deck. In the spring of 1730, the Rhode Island vessel, *Little George,* left the Guinea Coast. Somehow the African men slipped out of their chains, overpowered the crew, threw them overboard, and returned the ship to Africa. Many revolts were not as successful; it is estimated that 100 million Africans died resisting slavery.

Before Africans were sold to slave owners, they had to be "seasoned." Seasoning had four objectives: To make the slave fear the owner and fear death or torture for disobedience. To make the slave identify with and be loyal to the owner (even against fellow slaves). To make the slave believe that the White race was superior to the Black race (thereby justifying White people owning Black people). To make the slave hate Africa and anyone Black (again destroying the slave's pride).

In seasoning, Africans were sent to slavemakers or human-breakers — much like wild stallions are sent to horsebreakers to be trained to obey their owners. In this process, Africans were beaten, denied food and water, and humiliated in front of their families. This continued until their will to resist slavery was broken. The stronger a slave's will, the more brutal the season-ing. No, Africans' will to be free was not removed at Goree Island or during the two nightmarish months at sea; rather, many lost their wills during seasoning. It should be noted, however, that even despite seasoning, some slaves were never broken. Though they gave their masters the impression that they had been bro-ken, their will to resist remained intact. As we shall see later, many eventually escaped or rebelled.

One of the greatest tools in making a slave was fear. Whenever there was a beating or lynching, all the slaves were forced to witness it. This served as a warning to them in case they consid-ered disobeying. Most plantations and farms had more slaves than Whites. Control could only be maintained with guns, fear,

slave loyalty, and slaves hating themselves. There were many more slaves than Whites, but if Africans could be divided against each other, they could be conquered. Africans were rewarded generously for telling the owner about other Africans' plans for escape. Rewards included being made overseer or plantation supervisor, more food, and working and sleeping in the owner's house.

Africans were made to believe they were inferior by the use of White military strength, economic power, and the White image of Jesus. Whites rationalized that Africans were savages being saved by them. Money, guns, and the misuse of religion were all used to convince Africans of their inferiority.

Lastly, Africans were taught to hate their homeland and anything black. They were ridiculed about their skin color, hair texture, and facial features. White men presented their women as upholding the finest examples of beauty. African children who were products of slave owners and African women were called mulattoes. They were given special privileges similar to those that told owners about escape plans. Whites belittled African culture and told them Africa had made no contribution to the world in mathematics, science, literature, arts, architecture, etc. This can only occur when a people do not know their history.

After seasoning, slaves were placed on the auction block. They were sold like objects.

"Who will pay 500 dollars for a strong colored mandingo?" the auctioneers would say. He was then viewed like an animal. Potential buyers would look in his ears, mouth, anus, and over his sexual organs. If the buyer had doubts about the slave's health or strength, he would try to lower the price; but if satisfied, the bidding could reach thousands of dollars.

"Who will pay 500 dollars for this young, colored girl good for making baby slaves?" the auctioneer would say. She was just as valuable as the male slave if she passed the physical inspection. This one female could breed 10-15 more slaves and still work.

The African family tried to stay together. They pleaded with owners to buy their relatives. This was not a priority of the owners. If they needed the relatives and won the bidding, the family stayed together; but if they did not, the family was torn apart. Husbands, wives, and children screamed for each other. Many times, late at night, those screams would be the only and last sound they would hear from their loved ones as they were being sold—never to see each other again.

The African family has always been strong. During slavery, men and women risked their lives, running away from their masters in search of each other. Those families that were able to be sold together had to witness the humiliation each member received. Parents had to watch while their children were overworked and beaten. During slavery, marriage was not honored. Husbands had to watch while their wives were sexually abused by the owners. Women screamed louder than their husbands when they were beaten. They worked from sunrise to sunset or sixteen hours a day. Some of the crops produced were cotton, sugar, and tobacco.

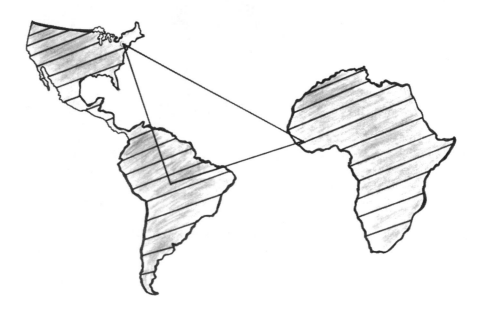

The Middle Passage or triangle included Africa, America, and the West Indies. There were many countries in South and Central America. Large numbers of Africans were shipped to Brazil, Jamaica, and Haiti. In most of these countries, Africans outnumbered Whites. For this reason, in the islands, mulattoes were classified as Whites to increase their numbers. One drop of white blood made you White, while in America where there were more

Whites, one drop of Black blood made you Black. Africans in the islands have been able to preserve more of their culture because of less European contact.

Work on the plantation was divided between the field and house. More of the workers labored in the fields. While work was hard in both locations, house work was physically easier and a slave could avoid the sun. Many light-skinned Africans worked in the house. Some loved their White fathers and hated their African mothers, while others felt the reverse. When the owner got sick many house slaves were sad, while field slaves rejoiced.

After working all day, many Africans would read under a candle or moonlight. They had to hide while reading, because the master was not in favor of Africans being educated. This should teach you the importance of an education. Why would the owner not want Africans to be educated? Many Africans remembered the Grand Lodge of Wa'at and the University of Sankore.

From Africa, to the boat, to the plantation many Africans never accepted slavery. To resist, many Africans worked no harder than they had to, put on deliberate work slow-downs, staged sit-down strikes, set fires to buildings and fields, broke tools, trampled crops, and at times, poisoned the slave owners.

Paul Cuffe, who had his name changed from that of his father's slave owner, who was named Slocum, was a shipowner.

Paul had very little confidence that America would change its evil ways and he planned to take his people back to Africa. In 1811, aboard his ship, the *Traveller,* he sailed from Massachusetts to Sierra Leone with thirty-eight Africans. This cost him 4,000 dollars of personal funds.

There were over 265 slave revolts primarily led by Christian ministers. They were responding to the oppressive codes that said slaves could not:

beat drums.

assemble in groups of more than five.

conduct religious service without a White present.

learn to read and write, or to buy and sell goods.

own property or testify in court.

possess firearms.

strike a White person.

Whites knew that "drum talk," a sophisticated form of communication, was often used to communicate information about escape or revolt. This reinforces the need for us to hold our musicians accountable to providing music that has a liberating message. The assembling of five or more posed a security problem that even today in Azania (South Africa) is being enforced. As previously mentioned, many of the slave revolts came out of the church. Whites saw the power from the church and wanted to monitor it. Owners were equally afraid of Africans learning how to read and compute, because a literate person can increase the use of forms of communication, and defend himself financially in the marketplace. Whites also did not want to acknowledge Africans as peers who were landowners and had rights in courts. They certainly did not want Africans equipped with weaponry, because that could lead to Africans attacking them.

The spirit of African-American resistance was best stated by David Walker in his appeal written in 1829. This self-taught scholar and writer for the first African-American newspaper, *Freedom's Journal,* published and distributed a 77-page radical document called the *Appeal,* that connected slavery with racism and capitalism. (Racism is the belief by a race that they are superior to other races, and is the ability to express that belief physically, economically, and politically. Capitalism is an economic system that values profit at the expense of human labor. The power lies with the ownership of capital.) Other leaders, before and after Walker, thought that merely ending slavery would end the oppression of African-Americans. Walker's book showed that racism and capitalism would continue to oppress African people even if slaves were freed. It showed how Africans who lived in some areas of the North, and were not slaves, were oppressed anyway. Walker also wrote that God was on the side of freedom and that His wrath would come upon those who would enslave others. Walker also demanded African unity between those free and those enslaved. He encouraged Africans to value education and self-defense measures.

White abolitionists spoke around the country attempting to influence Whites to abolish slavery. The Quakers aided Harriet Tubman and the Underground Railroad, providing safe places to hide, food, and other assistance. The American Anti-Slavery

Society, led by William Lloyd Garrison, made a nationwide thrust. John Brown led a group of Whites and Blacks in an insurrection at Harper's Ferry, Virginia with the intent of raiding the federal arsenal and distributing guns to Africans all over America.

Two of the most noted African-American leaders of the nineteenth Century were Frederick Douglass and Martin Delany. They both worked together on the newspaper called *The North Star.* Frederick Douglass, born a rebellious slave, was sent to slave makers often, but escaped to freedom at the age of twenty-one. He was taught by Whites and became an excellent writer and orator with Garrison and the American Anti-Slavery Society. Douglass said, "If there is no struggle, there is no progress."

Martin Delany was a gifted man. He was a doctor, writer, speaker, and military major. He named his son after Toussaint L'Ouverture, who led Haiti to independence. Delany was born

free, and his family instilled in him racial pride. He and Douglass worked well together, but they often disagreed. Douglass said, "I thank God for making me a man," but Delany said, "I thank him for making me a Black man." Delany, the author of the novel, *Blake,* recalled the ideas of David Walker's *Appeal* and saw slavery as being connected with racism and economic exploitation. He observed that in the American Anti-Slavery Society, of which Douglass was a member, and in similar groups, Whites were always in positions of leadership. Delany was an advocate of all African groups coming together to discuss liberation strategies. When the Fugitive Slave Act of 1850 was passed, placing in jeopardy the status of free Africans, Delany said, "If any man approaches my house in search of a slave, I care not who he may be, whether constable, sheriff, magistrate, or even judge of the Supreme Court, nay let it be President Millard Fillmore surrounded by his cabinet and bodyguard, with the Declaration of Independence waving above his head as his banner, and the constitution of his country upon his breast as his shield, if he crosses the threshhold of my door, and I do not lay him a lifeless corpse at my feet, I hope the grave may refuse my body a resting place, and righteous heaven my spirit a home. O, No! He cannot enter that house and we both live." In other words, Delany was saying fugitive slaves would be taken from his house "over his dead body."

In 1859, frustrated over the slave codes, Delany formed the Niger Valley Exploring Committee and went back to West Africa to discuss with African leaders the possibility of immigration. This, along with Paul Cuffe's movement, was the foundation of Pan-Africanism. Pan-Africanism is a philosophy that we are Africans wherever we live, Nigeria, Jamaica, or America, and that none of us are free until all of us are free. Therefore, Africans from around the world should come together to discuss our common problems and solutions. It is unfortunate that today's African-Americans know so little about Martin Delany.

Although the northern part of the United States was just as racist as the southern part of the United States, the southern part was more adamant about maintaining slavery. Why?

1. There were more states that allowed slavery in the South than in the North.
2. There were more states and more people in the South whose income and wealth were dependent on slave labor. There were more factories in the North than in the South. Factories could survive economically with cheap labor (workers who are paid substandard wages). Large plantations needed free labor (no wages paid) to survive.
3. There were more slaves in the South than in the North; therefore millions of freed slaves in the South would cause the southerners more of a problem than thousands of freed slaves in the North would cause the northerners.
4. Many northerners felt that the safety of the country was jeopardized by slave revolts such as the Harper's Ferry raid on a federal arsenal.
5. More White religious denominations which opposed slavery were based in the North.

When the differences over slavery and other issues intensified in the 1850's and 1860's, many slave states decided to secede from the United States, and start a new country — the Confederate States of America. The remaining states (also known as the Union or the North) were under the leadership of then-President of the United States, Abraham Lincoln. He sent the Army and Navy to prevent this seccession. The Confederate states fought back. This conflict became known as the Civil War or the War Between the States.

In order to get more Africans, as well as European countries (France and England, having long before outlawed slavery) to side with the Union in the war, Lincoln issued a document called the Emancipation Proclamation. It stated that all slaves in states that had seceded were free as of January 1, 1863. This proclamation did not free the 800,000 to one million Africans in the states that were still part of the Union. Because the Confederate states were at that time no longer part of the Union, the proclamation did not free slaves in those states. Most historians agree that the Emancipation Proclamation was thus not a humanitarian document, but was rather a part of the Union's wartime strategy to gain support. Abraham Lincoln, referred to by some as "The Great Emancipator" and as a "champion for human rights," simply was not. His words quoted below show his true feeling: "I am not, nor ever have I been in favor of bringing about, in any way, the social and political equality of the white and black races. I am not, nor ever have I been, in favor of making voters or jurors of Negroes, nor of qualifying them to hold office, nor to intermarry with white people; and I will say in addition to this that there is a physical difference between the white and black races which I believe will forever forbid the two races living together on terms of social and political equality. And insomuch as they cannot so live, while they do remain together, there must be the position of superior and inferior, and I as much as any other man am in favor of having the superior position assigned to the white race."

Bibliography

Young Adult
Frederick Douglass, Joseph Cinque and The Amistad Mutiny.
The Saga of Harriet Tubman, Golden Legacy Magazines, Seattle: Fitzgerald Publishing, 1983.
Adult
Frederick Douglass Institute. *Unpublished Social Studies Curriculum Guide,* St. Louis: 1987.
Bennett, Lerone. *Before the Mayflower.* Chicago: Johnson Publishing, 1962.
Gutman, Herbert. *The Black Family in Slavery and Freedom.* New York: Vintage, 1976.
Harding, Vincent. *There is a River.* New York: Harcourt Brace Jovanovich, 1981.

Vocabulary

Write the definition for each word. Write a sentence using each word. Draw a picture of your favorite word on the list or in the chapter.

Adamant	Indentured
Arsenal	Literate
Breed	Mulatto
Capitalism	Orator
Coast	Racism
Conducive	Secede
Document	Strategic
Immigration	Technology
	Viable

Questions

1. Why did Africans allow invaders to settle along the coast?
2. Compare the historical differences between European and African technology.
3. How was slavery different as practiced by Africans, Europeans, or Arabs?
4. How did Africans arrive in Jamaica and Haiti?
5. What were four things slave makers tried to teach Africans?
6. How did Africans express resistance to slavery?
7. Describe the efforts of Whites to abolish slavery.
8. Why is more information available on Douglass than on Delany?
9. How did Lincoln feel about Africans?
10. Describe Pan-Africanism.

Exercises

1. Write a paper to your ancestors, who did not commit suicide during the Middle Passage, and thank them for the opportunity you have to live.
2. Write a play about Africans allowing the invaders to settle along the coast.
3. Make an African triangle out of magazine pictures showing Africans living in Africa, the Caribbean, and America.
4. Write a play about seasoning.
5. Have oratorical exhibitions using Martin Delany's speech.
6. Write a play about the African family being sold separately.

Chapter Three

Strategies for Liberation

The Watch Tower services began late Saturday evening, December 31, 1862. African-Americans had already begun to take freedom into their own hands, but midnight would, from the White northern perspective, allow them to enlist in the Union Army. African-Americans were anxiously awaiting the arrival of 1863 all over the country. Churches still celebrate Watch Tower services on New Year's Eve to bring in the year. Many Africans in the South celebrate "Juneteenth" (June 19), because that's when they received the news of emancipation. There have been many laws that have affected African-Americans and a few of these laws include:

1787 - African-Americans are considered 3/5 a person, and viewed as property.

1850 - *The Fugitive Slave Act* places in jeopardy free Africans' status when traveling, and prevents slaves from believing that traveling north will keep them permanently free.

1857 - U.S. Supreme Court rules that Dred Scott, an African, is not a U.S. citizen, and therefore has no rights.

The Thirteenth, Fourteenth, and Fifteenth amendments (1866) respectively, ended slavery in all states, gave citizenship, and voter's rights. Reconstruction began with the right to vote. Reconstruction was an attempt by the federal government to aid African-Americans just released from slavery with the guaranteed right to vote. This was achieved with the assistance of federal troops.

Africans have always been concerned with government, from the Council of Elders to the political councils that worked with Queen Hatshepsut and King Ramses. After slavery, African-Americans were elected to local, state, and national offices. Between 1869 and 1901, two African-Americans from Mississippi served in the U.S. Senate. They were Hiram Revels and Blanche Bruce. Twenty were in the United States House of Representatives.

Today, there are over 5,000 African elected officials. Of these, about 25 serve in the United States Congress and over 100 serve as mayors of cities.

After the war, Africans asked, "free to do what? To go where? How?" The Freedman's Bureau, created in 1865, was designed to provide medical care, food, education, and economic development for four million African-Americans.

The Bureau helped create Howard, Fisk, Atlanta Universities, and Hampton Institute. The Black church grew in this period. The African Methodist Episcopal Church, founded by Richard Allen in 1787, grew from 20,000 in 1856 to 200,000 in 1876. The National Baptists grew from 150,000 to 500,000.

Congressman Thaddeus Stevens proposed "that forty acres and a mule" be given to African-Americans from southern lands won in the war by the North. Oliver Howard, the leader of the Freedmen's Bureau, had to announce there would be no land. The president at that time, Andrew Johnson, had changed his mind and sided with past southern owners. This created an uproar among African-Americans. Many of them physically resisted Whites taking back the land that some African-Americans had just begun to occupy. They publicly expressed their discontent, but it fell on deaf ears in the White House. Many African-Americans, who believe in reparations, still feel today the government has not kept its agreement.

The South was not used to Africans having citizenship. They were angry at the North for giving African-Americans positions in government. The Ku Klux Klan was founded during Reconstruction. They are a racist group that attempts to place fear in people with acts of violence. Previous White slave owners created all kinds of laws to reduce the effects of Reconstruction. For example, laws were passed that Africans could only vote if their grandfathers had voted, passed literacy tests, paid a poll tax, and could figure out when the office would be open. The grandfather law would eliminate most Africans from voting, because few Africans voted before 1865. The literacy tests would further reduce the number, because most owners had not allowed reading on the plantation. The poll tax connected income to voting, consequently poor people could not vote. Many Africans attempted to vote, but Whites would close the office when they saw Africans approaching.

For example, in 1896 there were 130,344 African-American voters in Louisiana. By 1900, after these new laws there were only 5,320. I hope you appreciate how much your ancestors endured for you to have the opportunity to vote.

Vagrancy laws were created that forced African-Americans to quit waiting on forty acres and a mule, and go back to work. These laws prevented Africans from owning or renting property. This new work relationship under contract or sharecropping paid Africans an inadequate wage or a share in the crop. Each form of payment denied Africans from becoming economically independent.

Booker T. Washington, born in 1856 and a graduate of Hampton Institute, said at the Atlanta Exposition of 1895, "I apologize for the errors my race made by beginning at the top instead of at the bottom, in seeking seats in state legislature rather than developing skills in industry and real estate. No race can grow until it learns that there is as much dignity in tilling a field as in writing a poem. Cast down your buckets where you are in agriculture, mechanics, and commerce, in all things that are social, we can be as separate as the fingers, yet one as the hand in all things essential for mutual progress."

Whites loved the speech because it seemed to call for reduced social and political involvement by African-Americans and provided a source of cheap labor. Washington helped develop the Negro Business League which led to the formation of The Urban League. He was also principal of Tuskegee, which he transformed from two buildings in 1881 to over 50 buildings when he died in 1915. He was considered by United States presidents and business executives as the African-American leader.

There was a segment of the African population, led by W.E.B. DuBois, that was not in agreement with Washington. DuBois who was born in 1868 and lived 95 years, was one of the founders of the National Association for the Advancement of Colored People (NAACP). DuBois, a graduate of Howard, professor at Atlanta University, author of twenty-two books, and editor of the *Crisis* magazine, believed in a liberal versus a vocational education. He designed a concept called the "Talented Tenth," which advocated that liberation strategies should come from scholars. Unlike Washington, DuBois felt strongly about participation in political and social activities.

DuBois coordinated the Pan-African Conference in Paris in 1919, and stated, "The problem of the twentieth century is the problem of color. This double-consciousness, this sense of always looking at one's self through the eyes of others, of measuring one's soul by the tape of a world that looks on in amused contempt and pity. One ever feels his twoness — An American, a Negro; two souls, two thoughts, two unreconciled strivings, two warring ideals in one dark body, whose dogged strength alone keeps it from being torn asunder." In other words, trying to feel good about being Black in a White world is very difficult.

After the death of Booker T. Washington, many Africans recognized W.E.B. DuBois as the leader of the African-American community.

The tension between Washington and DuBois is a historical repeat of Douglass and Delany. White people and the media choose our leaders, provide more favorable information about those leaders with whom Whites are more comfortable, and then we make ill-informed decisions about messengers rather than critically looking at the messages. Both Washington and DuBois wanted to improve the conditions of African people. The messages from Washington were economic development and educational institutions that taught technical and vocational skills. These are messages that we can still use today. The messages from DuBois were a liberal education, publishing, and political involvement locally, nationally and internationally. These are messages that we also can use today.

The Great Migration witnessed millions of African-Americans leaving the South. Prior to the Civil War, ninety percent of African-Americans lived in the South, while today the number hovers around fifty percent. The mass movement was precipitated by the end of Reconstruction and by World War I (1917-1918). The promise of jobs "up North" drove 50,000 African-Americans per year northward between 1910-1920. The South tried to harass and prevent northern personnel agents from recruiting African-American labor.

The end of the war and the Depression of 1929-1940 slowed the migration between 1920 and 1940, but from 1940 through 1960, 150,000 Africans per year relocated. Ninety percent of the migration went to the northeast and north central United States, but after 1940, twenty percent headed west, primarily to California.

Most African-Americans went by train; it was jokingly called the "Chickenbone Special," because most Africans couldn't afford to buy food on the train, so they brought chicken. They followed the direction of the railroad tracks. Those living in the Carolinas and Georgia went to New York, Philadelphia, Baltimore, and Washington, D.C. Those living in Mississippi, Alabama, and Tennessee went to Chicago, Detroit, Cleveland, and St. Louis. Africans living in Arkansas, Texas, and Oklahoma traveled to California.

The Harlem Renaissance rivals any period of any race in terms of excellence in fine arts. The Great Migration brought a wealth of talent from rural to urban areas. No place generated more of this vitality than Harlem in New York City.

Some of the writers associated with this period included Langston Hughes, Claude McKay, Countee Cullen, Jean Toomer, Alaine Locke, James Weldon Johnson, and Zora Neale Hurston.

Carter G. Woodson, educator and historian, founded Negro History Week, the second week in February, in honor of Frederick Douglass' birthday. This has grown now to become a month-long celebration called Black Liberation Month.

Playing at the Sunset and Cotton Clubs were Duke Ellington, Louis Armstrong, Eubie Blake, Bessie Smith, and Billie Holliday. W.C. Handy's musical spirituals brought inspiration to a concerned people. Katherine Dunham and her majestic feet had everyone doing dances of the period including the "Charleston," "Black Bottom," and "Shuffle Along." Paul Robeson stunned people on stage. Henry Ossawa Tanner captured in art what others could only dream. Many of the songs, poems, novels, and the art of this time had themes of African pride, unity, and resistance to oppression. The Harlem Renaissance thus caused many people to think about their condition in this country, and to press for true freedom. Something else happened during this period which caused Africans to think and press for freedom — World War I. People who fought in this war were told they were fighting for the freedom of European countries. These were the same countries who met in 1880 in Berlin to divide Africa according to their own interests. Many African-Americans who returned from this war began to think, "If the United States can fight for other nations' freedom, why won't it grant my people freedom in the United States?" Also, they thought, "If I can fight for European nations' freedom, I should fight for and expect my people's freedom in the United States." Yes, it was very difficult for these returning African-Americans to accept the same type of treatment they got prior to the war.

Another factor in this period that stimulated African-Americans to press for freedom was the "Red Summer" of 1919, during which 83 African-Americans were lynched. Lynching was death by hanging, burning, or other mob violence. At least 3,436 documented cases of lynching occurred from 1889 through 1922.

"Up you mighty race, you can accomplish what you will," proudly extorted Marcus Garvey during the 1920's. Garvey, born in August 1887 and later invited from Jamaica to America by Booker T. Washington, created the slogan, "Black is Beautiful" and proudly displayed the Shrine of Black Madonna in his African Orthodox Church. Garvey was the founder of the Universal Negro Improvement Association (UNIA), consisting of one million members and a following of over six million.

Garvey, like Washington, believed in economic development and created a newspaper, *The Negro World.* The UNIA also founded the Factory Corporation, a combination of stores and service enterprises, and The Black Star Line, a steamship corporation with the objective of returning Africans to Africa. Garvey felt Africans would never receive justice in America and advocated returning home. Garvey organized the African Legion, which was a military group intended to remove the invaders occupying Africa. After the Berlin Conference, European countries had divided Africa into separate colonies according to Europeans' own economic and military interests. Garvey, in the tradition of Paul Cuffe and Martin Delany, said, "Africa for the Africans," which meant Africa belongs to Africans, not to invaders for their exploitation. He developed the Liberation Flag which contained red, black, and green colors. Like Washington, Garvey appealed more to lower income African-Americans.

While Garvey and Washington had similar economic ideas, Garvey was not compromising to Whites, and connected his business interests to Africa, self-defense, education, and a redefinition of beauty based on African images. The historical tension

between messengers was played out again, but not between Garvey and Washington. Washington died before Garvey arrived in America. The tension existed between Garvey and DuBois. The one leader syndrome had both leaders arguing with each other, with Whites and their controlled media giving more favorable information about DuBois. DuBois accused Garvey of being dictatorial and a poor businessman. Garvey felt DuBois valued appealing to Whites for equal opportunity, more than creating businesses. The larger African community, caught between *messengers,* often missed the significance of the *messages.*

Elijah Muhammad was born Elijah Poole. He was a follower of Marcus Garvey and became the leader of the Nation of Islam (N.O.I.) in 1933. The Nation began in 1930 with the splitting into two factions of the Moorish Science Temple. One faction followed the founder, Noble Drew Ali, and the remaining members were loyal to W. Fard Muhammad who disappeared in 1933.

Elijah Muhammad, son of a sharecropper and minister, was born in 1897, and became Muhammad's chief assistant. He synthesized the principles of the Moorish Science Temple and Garvey to build the Nation of Islam. The N.O.I. believed in God, justice, and equality. They believed women should be respected and protected and that African children should be taught by African teachers. The N.O.I. believed in a separate state or territory that was fertile and minerally rich. This institution grew to own over forty temples or mosques, had 250,000 members, published the weekly *Muhammad Speaks* newspaper, developed the Clara Muhammad Schools, secured farmland, and operated stores and service enterprises nationwide.

Messenger Muhammad instilled racial pride through the religion of Islam. He also aroused his audiences with a condemnation of Whites and connected their oppression of Africans to the work of the devil. This radical Islamic theology and ideology in a country controlled by Whites and populated with many Christians attracted large numbers, especially low income men. Prisons were a major source for recruits and the Fruit of Islam (the male group within the N.O.I.) became a shining example of how wayward African males could become strong African men.

The period between 1933 and 1963 is considered the Civil Rights Era. The first boycott was instituted in New York with the slogan, "Don't buy where you can't work." A boycott is an organized consumers' response to refuse to patronzie where there is unfairness. There were many "Jim Crow" laws that African-Americans wanted to change. Jim Crow laws supported segregation, and provided better goods and services for Whites than for African-Americans. There were separate toilets, water fountains, parks, schools, libraries, theatres, and restaurants for Blacks and Whites.

On December 2, 1955, Rosa Parks, a secretary for the NAACP and a seamstress, boarded a Montgomery, Alabama bus and sat in the front. This was considered okay unless a White person needed a seat because the front of a bus was filled. Eventually, the bus filled and Mrs. Parks was asked to move to the back. She refused. It was not the first time African-Americans had refused to move or obey other Jim Crow laws. What made this significant was that Rosa Parks said, "My feet were tired," and like Fannie Lou Hamer, another leader of the Civil Rights Era who often said, "I'm sick and tired of being sick and tired," Mrs. Parks was arrested, but the African-American community responded in protest.

African-Americans had just won *Brown* vs. *Board of Education* (1954), reversing *Plessey* vs. *Ferguson* (1896) (separate but equal), and the Supreme Court declared that separate but equal public schools were unconstitutional. Jim Crow laws had reinforced *Plessey* vs. *Ferguson*, and while the facilities were separate, they were not equal. African-Americans believed that with their victory of *Brown* vs. *Topeka*, segregation in schools would

end, and all children would be taught together and receive equal resources. This decision inspired Africans to break Jim Crow laws on buses, in restaurants, parks, etc.

A group of ministers formed the Montgomery Improvement Association and asked if Rev. Martin Luther King, Jr. would be the president. They formed carpools, conducted church services every evening and for 381 days boycotted the Montgomery bus company until they conceded to hiring African-American drivers and a first-come-first-serve basis for seating on buses.

Martin Luther King, Jr., born in 1929 and a graduate of Morehouse College during the presidency of educator Benjamin Mays, received his doctorate in theology from Boston University and entered the same profession as his father. This civil rights leader was jailed thirty times during his career. In 1963 he led 100,000 people on the March on Washington. The following year he was honored with the Nobel Peace Prize and a $54,000 check that he contributed to the Southern Christian Leadership Council (SCLC), founded by him in 1957. This contribution is significant because it shows King's dedication to the liberation of his people. We have many athletes and entertainers who spend most of their money on several mansions and luxurious cars, and very little for the liberation of their people. The father of four children and

husband to Coretta, King advocated nonviolent resistance and led the Civil Rights Era with a four-pronged attack of boycotts, sit-ins, freedom rides, and mass marches. A sit-in is an organized group that occupies as many seats as possible at a public facility or a place of business such as a lunch counter which will not serve Africans. The sit-in eliminates or reduces the number of Whites that can be served, and it disrupts the usual business activity so attention can be drawn to the unfair and illegal practice that usually takes place. The objective was to force the owner to realize it was easier to serve them, so the seats could be freed up for White customers. Freedom rides were conducted by organized groups in an attempt to force interstate bus companies to let African-Americans ride. In the past, Whites stopped individual riders, but this organized effort made it more difficult. Mass marches were large demonstrations of people designed to show oppressors unity, and an opportunity to inform larger numbers of Africans of the pertinent issues.

What made the Civil Rights Era more effective was the advent of television into American homes. A nationwide audience saw White governors, mayors, and police officers beating, hosing, and using dogs and tear gas on innocent women and children.

The Student Nonviolent Coordinating Committee (SNCC), led by Stokley Carmichael (now known as Kwame Ture), H. Rap Brown, James Foreman, and Fannie Lou Hamer led the sit-ins at lunch counters all over the South. They were beaten at the counter, spit on by waitresses, and had food thrown in their faces. They were often arrested after they were beaten for disturbing the peace, but the students never quit and more sat at lunch counters the next day. Kwame Ture, who has been a consistent advocate for the liberation of African people, inspired them with the charge, "Black Power."

The Congress on Racial Equality (CORE), led by James Farmer, sent freedom riders across the South in efforts to integrate buses traveling nationwide. These riders, Black and White, were also beaten, three were killed, and buses were burned.

The pressure of SCLC, SNCC, and CORE boycotting, sitting-in, riding, and marching — all shown on national and international television—forced Congress to pass and United States President Lyndon Johnson to sign the most far-reaching civil rights legislation in the history of the country in 1965. The men and women — Black and White — that were beaten, hosed, bitten, and killed did it so that you and I could be free.

Martin Luther King, Jr., who denounced Jim Crow and U.S. involvement in Vietnam, got his strength from God and stood up to America without fear.

In one of his sermons, King said: "The only way we can really achieve freedom is to somehow conquer the fear of death. But if a man has not discovered something that he will die for, he isn't fit to live. Deep down in our nonviolent creed is the conviction there are some things so dear, some things so precious, some things so eternally true that they are worth dying for, and if a man happens to be 36 years old, as I happen to be, and some great truth stands before the door of his life, some great opportunity to stand up for that which is right and that which is just, and he refuses to stand up because he wants to live a little longer, and he's afraid his home will get bombed, or he's afraid that he will lose his job, or he's afraid that he will get shot or beat down by state troopers, he may go on and live until he's 80, but he's just as dead at 36 as he would be at 80 and the cessation of breathing in his life is merely the belated announcement of an earlier death of the spirit. Man dies when he refuses to stand up for that which is right. A man dies when he refuses to stand up for justice."

Malcolm X had a strong Black man as a father. His father was a Garvey follower and minister who was killed by the Klu Klux Klan. Malcolm, born in 1925, was taken from relative to relative, from Lansing, to Boston, Detroit, and eventually to New York. He was a dropout and became a pimp and hustler, earning the nickname "Detroit Red," because of his hair and street sense.

He got caught and went to jail from 1946 through 1952. His brothers, Wilfred and Reginald, both Muslims, introduced him to the literature of Elijah Muhammad. Malcolm corresponded with Muhammad and upon release became an assistant minister in Detroit. He became a minister in Philadelphia and New York. The father of four daughters and husband to Betty, he electrified audiences with his honesty and attracted crowds the size of those attracted by Marcus Garvey. Malcolm X said: "The Key to our success lies in united action. Lack of unity has always been the reason we have failed to win concrete gains in our war against oppression. My Black brothers and sisters of all religious beliefs, or of no religious beliefs — we all have a common enemy, and the greatest binding tie we could have...we are all Black people, as Black people we must unite." His messages were racial pride, economic development, securing land, and operating schools.

He was critical of Martin Luther King's nonviolent philosophy and advocated self-defense. In 1964, he made his pilgrimage to Mecca, and saw Muslims of all races in brotherhood. He also visited Africa twice that year, and saw Africans, both Christians and Muslims, working together. The government, via the FBI and led by J. Edgar Hoover and the United States President, carefully watched African-American organizations and were always investigating Malcolm X and King. Malcolm wanted to appeal to the United Nations for human not just civil rights. Martin Luther King began speaking against United States' involvement in Vietnam. Civil rights are issues that pertain to citizenship within a national border. Human rights are not confined by citizenship, geography, race, gender or religion. Malcolm X and Doctor King initially responded to issues concerning Africans only in the United States, but when these two men began expanding their ideology to international issues such as the Vietnam War, colonialism, and imperialism (foreign countries who control the labor and natural resources directly or with leaders they've influenced), they became unacceptable to the ruling White class. The possibility of both men expanding their base and communicating with each other was too much for oppressors to allow — therefore they were killed.

The movement for liberation continues today. Jesse Jackson was a follower of Dr. King. Operation Push, founded by Jackson, is an outgrowth of Operation Breadbasket which Martin Luther King founded. Louis Farrakhan was a follower of Elijah Muhammad. He is continuing the building of the Nation of Islam. Jackson continues King's message of boycotting and mass marches. Jackson has also formed the Rainbow Coalition consisting of Africans, Hispanics, Asians, Native Americans, women, and the White working and poor classes. He believes the presidency of the United States should be occupied by other people and not confined to just White men. Farrakhan continues Muhammad's message of economic development with the newspaper, *The Final Call,* and the distribution of fish. He has added "Power" products which include soap, shampoo, lotion, toothpaste, and other toiletries. Farrakhan is also trying to unify ministers of all faiths in the quest for total African liberation. Many people and institutions, particularly the media, try to separate Jackson from Farrakhan, King from Malcolm, Douglass from Delany, and eliminate Garvey and Muhammad from history.

The powers of this country want Africans to make choices with limited information. Most people know more about Jackson, King, and Douglass than they do about Farrakhan, Malcolm, Muhammad, Garvey, and Delany.

All of these messengers want Africans to be free to reach their full potential. Their messages include racial pride, economic development, securing land, operating schools, Pan-Africanism, self-defense, liberal and vocational education, publishing, boycotts, sit-ins, marches, freedom rides, and political involvement locally, nationally, and internationally.

49

The struggle for freedom has continued in Africa. African nations each year fought European countries over the right to self-determination. Five examples of African strength were the liberation struggles in Ghana, Tanzania, Zaire, Kenya, and Mozambique. The masses of Africans have been represented by Kwame Nkrumah, Julius Nyerere, Patrice Lumumba, Jomo Kenyatta, and Robert Mugabe respectively and won important victories. African nations saw they had a common enemy and in 1963 formed the Organization of African Unity (OAU).

The struggle for freedom continues in the African triangle, from America, the West Indies, and Africa. In Azania (South Africa) four million Europeans have control over twenty-two million Africans. They implemented a system called apartheid which gives special privileges to Europeans and forces Africans to live under inhuman conditions. Africans there do not have the right to vote.

The African National Congress and other groups continue to fight for freedom. Nelson Mandela, the recognized Azanian leader, was imprisoned in 1961 for his battle against apartheid. He was released in 1990, almost thirty years later. Bishop Desmond Tutu, who won the Nobel Peace Prize in 1984, is trying to reduce the violence in the quest for freedom. The United States government says they are in favor of democracy all over the world, but this government has done very little in aiding Africans to secure democracy in Azania. Large United States corporations continue to conduct business, and America imports valuable natural resources from Azania, including gold and diamonds.

Bibliography

Young Adult

The Life of Martin Luther King. Golden Legacy Magazine, Seattle: Fitzgerald Publishing, 1983.

Dennis, Denise. *Black History for Beginners.* New York: Writers and Readers Publishing, 1984.

Taifa, Nkechi. *Shining Legacy.* Washington: House of Songhay II, 1983.

Adult

Adams, Russell. *Great Negroes Past and Present.* Chicago: Afro-Am Publishing, 1963.

Banks, James. *March Toward Freedom.* Belmont: Fearon Pittman Publishers, 1978.

Bell, Janet. *Famous Black Quotations.* Chicago: Sabayt Publications, 1986.

Davis, Allison. *Leadership, Love and Aggression.* New York: Harcourt, 1983.

Franklin, John Hope. *From Slavery to Freedom.* New York: Knopf, 1947.

Muhammad, Elijah. *Message to the Blackman.* Chicago: Muhammad Mosque, 1965.

X, Malcolm. *Autobiography of Malcolm X.* New York: Grove, 1964.

Vocabulary

Write the definition for each word. Write a sentence using each word. Draw a picture of your favorite word on the list or in the chapter.

Advocate	Commerce	Economic
Apartheid	Conference	Government
Asunder	Consider	Hovers
Boycott	Contempt	Ideology
Citizen	Council	Institution
Civil	Dictator	Jeopardy

Legislature	Oppressor	Renaissance
Liberal	Pilgrimage	Reparations
Liberate	Population	Resist
Literacy	Radical	Scholar
Method	Reconstruction	Segment
Migration	Recruit	Theology
		Vagrancy
		Wage

Questions

1. List and describe the laws affecting Africans between 1787 and 1965.
2. What was the role of the Freedman's Bureau?
3. How did the South end Reconstruction?
4. What were the similarities and differences between Booker T. Washington and W.E.B. DuBois?
5. Describe the Harlem Renaissance.
6. What were the similarities and differences between Booker T. Washington and Marcus Garvey?
7. What is the N.O.I.?
8. What were the four strategies in the Civil Rights Era?
9. What messages did Malcolm X offer?
10. What were the similarities between Malcolm X and Doctor King?
11. Why were King and Malcolm killed?
12. Why do you think more information is given about Jackson, King, and Douglass than about Farrakhan, Malcolm, Muhammad, Garvey, and Delany?
13. Describe apartheid in Azania.

Exercises

1. Develop a panel discussion between the followers of Washington, DuBois, and Garvey.
2. Draw a map of the migrations going northeast, north central, and west.
3. Have students present several of Doctor King's and Malcolm's speeches.
4. Have students select their favorite message, create an election with campaign speeches, and conduct actual voting.

Chapter Four

We Call Them Brave

King Ramses (1328 - 1232 B.C. est.)

Pharaoh Ramses II is considered by many African historians as one of the greatest Egyptian kings. His reign was longer than any other; he built more structures, and brought peace to a war torn land. The Hittites, or Asians, had fought the Egyptians for twenty years. Ramses in one battle was surrounded and separated from his other division. He said a prayer, kept on fighting, and received help from the flank. He negotiated a peace treaty between Egyptians and Asians that also affected the surrounding region.

The son of Seti I, father to Meremptah, both king and husband to Queen Nefetara; he led Egypt for 66 years. During his administration, Africans thrived, and more temples and tombs were

built than in any other period. The temple at Abu-Simbel, which is the largest in the world, is in worship to God and meets all the requirements of a world wonder.

Hannibal (247 - 183 B.C.)

At the age of nine, Hannibal recited this oath to his father, Hamilcar, "I swear upon the Gods that as long as I live that I will never be a friend of the Romans." The ambassador of Rome said, "Carthage must be destroyed." The sides were chosen and for 22 years and three Punic wars, Hannibal defended his oath.

Hannibal ruled Cathage, the famous city of antiquity in North Africa, that claimed a million people at its zenith. The great city of agriculture, and international trade of its mineral resources was the envy of Rome. Hannibal did not have the numbers of the Romans or the equipment, but he had tremendous determination. He once surprised the Romans by crossing the snow-covered Alps, which had never been done before. He attempted this maneuver with 40,000 men, lost half of them, but defeated the Romans at the Tecenus River. His greatest victory was at Cannae with 32,000 men against 90,000 Romans. He deceived the Romans into the center and surrounded them in an ambush.

Queen N'Zinga (1582 - 1663)

Queen N'Zinga represents the strength of African people. She fought against the Portuguese for forty years over her country, Angola. The Portuguese used every trick against Africans to divide and conquer. They sold them guns for slaves, made slaves fight for them, and created friction between chiefs. N'Zinga's brother, who was a weak king, asked N'Zinga to represent him at the Luanda Treaty of 1622. She had been already fighting against them for six years. At this meeting, the Portuguese did not provide her a seat, and her men used their own bodies for the Queen.

She refused the Portugueses' terms. When her brother died, she became the official Queen and declared Angola free. This infuriated the Portuguese who tried to manipulate Africans to kill her. Instead, she infiltrated their ranks and won victory after victory. Her quick attacks became legendary from 1616 to 1656.

Toussaint L'Ouverture (1746 - 1803)

L'Ouverture's father was very proud of his son despite his

being born into slavery, and made sure that Toussaint learned how to read and acquire certain skills. L'Ouverture became very interested in herbs for healing and military strategy. His family lived on the island of Santo Domingo, in Haiti. This wealthy island was the attraction of England, Spain, and France.

Africans, who outnumbered the invaders, wanted to remove them from the island. L'Ouverture joined the army and became chief medical officer. He also taught soldiers military protocol and strategy. Toussaint took advantage of his medical background and knowledge of his homeland, and defeated Napoleon's 60,000 army with 20,000 men. He did this by extending the battle while the French were suffering from yellow fever.

L'Ouverture, which means "opener," became general and governor of Santo Domingo, now known as the Dominican Republic. His rise to general and governor resulted from his popularity and military victories. Napoleon was furious with the possibility of treating L'Ouverture as an equal. During the negotiation, L'Ouverture trusted France, and was taken prisoner. His second general, Jacques Dessalines, continued the fight; an African maid who heard of Napoleon's plans was able to inform Dessalines in sign language. Santo Domingo and Haiti became free.

Chaka (1786 - 1836)

Chaka showed great courage at a young age. He killed a dangerous snake at thirteen and a leopard at nineteen. He became leader of the Zulu empire at the age of 26. Often called Chaka Zulu or the Great Elephant, he brought great respect to the Zulu kingdom. He was a strict disciplinarian, and was very hard on his troops if they made mistakes.

He was a great fighter and during his reign, he introduced a special knife called the "assegai," which was more effective than a spear. He designed a larger shield which gave better protection. Chaka also developed a military strategy in which his first flank was shaped in a crescent and the reserves followed in parallel. The people of Azania are calling upon the spirit of Chaka Zulu in their quest to end apartheid's White supremacy.

Joseph Cinque (1811 - 1879)

Cinque was born into a royal family in the country of Sierra Leone. Prince Cinque, married and with three children, was kid-

napped by the invaders in 1839 and taken to Havana, Cuba. He and 48 others were placed on the *Amistad* for the final destination, the Island of Principe. Cinque was able to pull loose a nail from the ship plank and maneuver his chains free.

Cinque freed the others, and together they surprised the crew late at night after a storm, and killed everyone but the two owners. Cinque and others knew they needed the owners to navigate the *Amistad* back to Africa. The owners steered the ship east back to Africa by day and northwest back to America at night. This zigzag course took 63 days and led them to Long Island, New York. Cinque with ten men less who died of starvation, fought the Americans before being captured. Two years later, and after many court trials, the judge ruled that Cinque and the other African survivors were free to return home to Africa.

Nat Turner (1800 - 1831)

Nat Turner was a man with a calling. He read very well and became a minister. He represents a tradition of Christian minis-

ters who led over 265 slave revolts. He had escaped from South-
ampton, Virginia, before and stayed away for over thirty days.
Because of his spiritual commitment, his freedom was not as
important to him as was freeing his people and ending slavery.

He had read David Walker's *Appeal,* and had planned an
insurrection on July 4, but he became ill. On August 21, 1831, Nat
Turner and six men attacked the Turner plantation and killed
the entire family. The revolt now with 60 people and rising, continued to kill slave owners throughout the region until 55 were
dead. Word passed like wildfire, and troops and other White
families surrounded Nat Turner's men. Nat Turner was able to
escape capture for six more weeks, often burying himself in the
soil.

Harriet Tubman (1820 est. - 1913)

At the young age of fourteen, Harriet became a freedom fighter. A slave owner threw a brick at an African trying to escape.
Harriet jumped in between and was hit in the head. Throughout
her life, she suffered from headaches and periods of deep sleep.
Later, she ran away and followed the North Star to Philadelphia.

She contacted the Quakers, who had already helped to establish the Underground Railroad. This was a secret means of transportation where Quakers and others provided housing for runaway Africans. Concerned about her people, she returned to the South 19 times, bringing up 300 free Africans over the two hundred mile journey, which earned her the nickname, Moses. When clouds covered the North Star, she looked for mold on a tree. She knew the mold was on the north side. When some African men and women were tired and wanted to turn back, Harriet would put a gun to their head and say, "Dead men tell no tales — You go on or die." Slave owners hated Harriet Tubman and offered a $40,000 reward for her capture, dead or alive. She was never caught.

Nat Love "Deadwood Dick" (1856 - 1900)

The migrations from the South did not always go north and east. The gold rush of the 1850's and the expanding western part of the country brought many cowboys. Often, television and books talk about White cowboys and John Wayne, and omit 5,000

African American cowboys, and the greatest of them all, Deadwood Dick.

Nat Love won his nickname in a shooting contest. There were cowboys from all over, but "Deadwood Dick" won by hitting 8 of 10 bull's-eyes. "Deadwood Dick" was also a very good horse rider. He won many rodeos and roped wild mustangs. Nat Love was a herder and drove cattle all over the West, fighting outlaws along the way.

Muhammad Ali (1942 -)

The heavyweight title has always been a prize possession and when Jack Johnson and Joe Louis took the title from Whites, there was more than a championship at stake. Cassius Clay grew up as a boxer, winning the Golden Gloves in 1959, the Olympics in 1960, and the heavyweight crown in 1964. He became a Muslim in 1964, began learning from Elijah Muhammad, and changed his name to Muhammad Ali. He was not the typical boxer with all brawn and no brains; Ali was literate, communicative, and fought with his body, mind and soul.

He promoted his fights and backed up what he said. He told Joe Frazier, "I float like a butterfly and sting like a bee."

When America wanted to draft him for the Vietnam War, he refused because of his religion. Then his title was taken from him, he was sent to jail and he was denied the opportunity to earn millions of dollars, robbed of three vital years of his career, but his dignity remained. Muhammad Ali was a fighter. In 1970, three years later, the court allowed him to fight again, and Muhammad Ali went on to become the champion two more unprecedented times.

America has had many wars. The very first was between European prisoners who were released to America and England. African-Americans have always hoped that fighting on behalf of America for the cause of freedom would bring about reciprocity

for their freedom. America before World War I only used Africans when they had no other chance of winning.

In the Revolutionary War of 1776, George Washington (a former slave owner) only agreed to use Africans when England was going to use them against him. Five thousand African-Americans fought in the war, with Crispus Attucks being the first to die. Abraham Lincoln only signed the Emancipation Proclamation to free slaves from the Confederate states (over which he had no legal jurisdiction), so they could enlist with the Union Army. Major Delany and 186,000 Africans fought in the Civil War. Harriet Tubman was a nurse and a scout. She and eight other scouts along with 150 African troops raided the Confederates, freed 800 Africans, and secured thousands of dollars worth of supplies.

There were 367,000 Africans who fought in World War I, but General Benjamin Davis, Sr. did not become the first African-American general until 1940.

In World War II, 900,000 African-Americans fought in the war led by the fine example of Dorie Miller. The young sailor was aboard the ship bombed by the Japanese at Pearl Harbor. He jumped to a machine gun and shot down four Japanese planes. An officer had to order him to leave the ship because it was sinking. At the time he served as a mess attendant, the only position opened to African sailors.

While the Ku Klux Klan hid behind sheets, fighting only when the numbers were in their favor, the Tuskegee Airmen including Benjamin Davis, Jr. and 600 pilots destroyed 261 planes, and received 82 awards. Segregation ended in the military in 1948. The recent movie "Platoon" does not show the bravery or the disproportionate number of Africans in Vietnam. There were 22,000 African-Americans in Vietnam per year between 1965 and 1972. Africans were placed more on the front line, and casualties were higher among Africans in a war in which Martin Luther King felt America should not be involved.

The problems of unemployment have unfortunately led many African-Americans to choose this hazardous occupation. The Vietnam War was not fought to provide democracy to South Vietnam, but was the United States' and Russia's obsession to carve up the world for their own economic exploitation. The Vietnam War was a prelude to the next war, which will probably be fought in countries with people of color. There is a good possibility that this war could take place in Africa or the Caribbean. Remember, the Japanese were placed in concentration camps during World War II. Will you fight against your own people? Will you kill your brothers and sisters because you need a job?

Bibliography

Young Adult

Black Cowboys, The Saga of Toussaint L'Ouverture, Crispus Attucks. Golden Legacy Magazine. Seattle: Fitzgerald Publishing, 1983.

Olomenji. *Great Black Military Heroes*. Chicago: New Frontiers Unlimited Press, 1983.

Adult

Ali, Muhammad. *The Greatest, My Own Story*. New York: Random House, 1975.

Vocabulary

Write the definition for each word. Write a sentence using each word. Draw a picture of your favorite word on the list or in the chapter.

Antiquity	Navigate
Conquer	Negotiate
Flank	Official
Friction	Parallel
Herbs	Protocol
Infiltrate	Quest
Insurrection	Reciprocity
Island	Reign
Legend	Tradition
Literate	Treaty
Maneuver	Thrive
Military	Vital
	Zenith

Questions

1. Why was Ramses II considered a great king?
2. How was Hannibal able to defeat the Romans with less men?
3. Describe the leadership of Queen N'Zinga.
4. What was L'Ouverture's mistake with France?
5. Describe the military contributions of Chaka.
6. How did Cinque return back to Africa?
7. What do you think inspired Nat Turner?
8. Describe the Underground Railroad journey.
9. How many African-American cowboys headed west and who was the greatest?

10. What made Muhammad Ali a different kind of fighter?
11. Why have African-Americans fought the United States' wars?
12. Will you fight for America against your people in Africa? Explain.

Exercises

1. Play chess or checkers and show Hannibal's strategy.
2. Develop a skit illustrating the scene in 1622 between Queen N'Zinga and the Portuguese king.
3. Have a martial arts demonstration emphasizing self-defense.
4. Conduct a discussion on gangs and crime in the students' community.
5. Conduct a nature hike similar to the journeys taken along the Underground Railroad, and determine directions by the mold on trees, the position of the sun, and a compass.
6. Invite a Vietnam War veteran to speak to the class.

Chapter Five

The African Contribution

Africans have always been good in math and science. Originating in the Grand Lodge of Wa'at were the laws of geometry to build pyramids. Africans designed an iron smelting furnace that made steel, and they developed a lunar calendar. The Dogon of Mali mastered astronomy as they plotted the orbits of stars circling Sirius. From Imhotep to Walter Massey, Africans invented the lawn mower, stove, and refrigerator, fountain pen, pencil sharpener, and papyrus, which is the original paper. The slogan "The real McCoy," honors the greatness of Elijah McCoy. Almost everything we touch, Africans made a contribution.

Science, and particularly inventing, means very little if ideas are not protected, and capital is unavailable for further research

and product development. Many African-Americans were denied the ability to secure patents for their inventions, because of slavery and Jim Crow laws. Some Africans were tricked into sharing their findings with White inventors. Other Africans simply could not afford to pay for a patent. Many Africans wanted to keep their inventions and start their own enterprises. The lack of capital, and customer support, and business skills were major obstacles. African ideas were often stolen, underpaid, or ignored by White society.

Imhotep (3000 - 2920 B.C. est.)

Imhotep is the father of medicine. Medical students take an oath in his honor. (The oath is in Chapter 1.) Imhotep also designed the first pyramid called the Step Pyramid of Sakhara in 2780 B.C. He was a great doctor and created the first hospital in Egypt. The process of mummification or preparing the body for the "after-life" required surgery of the vital organs. Imhotep is considered the first surgeon and Hippocrates studied his works.

Benjamin Banneker (1731 - 1806)

Benjamin Banneker loved math and science and was educated in a Quaker school. Farmers from the surrounding area visited Banneker to determine the best time to plant. Banneker had already established his love for astronomy, the study of the stars and celestial bodies, and its impact on agriculture.

Banneker made the first clock in America by taking apart a watch with a knife, learning the function of each instrument, enlarging them, and placing them in a wooden frame.

Once, when Banneker was not studying the stars or repairing tools, he fell in love with Anola, who was a slave. Benjamin tried to buy her freedom unsuccessfully, and in an attempt to physically free her, she was killed. Banneker, who did not recover emotionally, buried himself in his work, and never married.

Banneker and five others were commissioned by the government to survey and design the nation's capital in Washington. When L'Enfant, the chief engineer, abruptly left the project with the plans, it appeared doomed. Banneker reconstructed the plans from memory to the amazement of everyone. He was praised as a genius. Banneker returned to Maryland to finish his lifelong project, an almanac. It was published in 1792, and became the

first science book written by an African in America. Banneker's *Almanac* received international acclaim and historically connected him with the Dogon of Mali and Imhotep.

Jan Matzeliger (1852 - 1889)

Before Jan Matzeliger designed the shoe lasting machine, skilled craftsmen could only produce 40 shoes per day, and they were very expensive. The "hand lasters" had to manually sew the upper shoe to the sole. In the fall of 1880, Matzeliger built a model shoe lasting machine out of hardware bits. He was offered fifty dollars, which he refused. Matzeliger constructed a larger model and was offered $1,500, but he refused again.

He secured financing for his machine and began producing shoes ten times faster than the manual process. Matzeliger developed tuberculosis six years after his invention and died. By 1889, the demand for his shoe lasting machine was international. Companies formed that emerged from his labor. The United Shoe Machinery Corporation and the industry has annual sales of four billion dollars.

Lewis Latimer (1848 - 1928)

After the Civil War, Latimer applied to be an office boy in a patent attorney's office. He worked very hard and became a draftsman. His reputation became known, and he was asked by Alexander Bell to draw the plans for the telephone. Latimer invented the process of manufacturing carbon filaments, which is the material in a light bulb that glows when electric current flows through. Previously, filaments were expensive, dangerous, and had poor longevity.

Hiram Maxim who owned the Electric Light Company in London, hired Latimer to set up a factory to produce carbon filaments. In 1890, he wrote the first book on electric lighting, and created parallel versus series circuiting. The former method avoided a blowout of all the lights if one was malfunctioning. Thomas Edison hired him as a expert witness in battles over patents. He became the only African in the Edison Pioneers.

Granville Woods (1856 - 1910)

Alexander Bell and Thomas Edison are indebted to Granville Woods. The original telephone could barely be heard, and not over long distances. Woods designed a transmitter that improved the quality of sound, and over longer distances.

Woods invented a telegraphony, a combination telephone and telegraph that allowed telegraph stations to send oral and signal messages over the same line. This eliminated telegraph operators having to know Morse code. He also introduced an electrically heated egg incubator, which made it possible to hatch 50,000 eggs at one time.

The transportation system could not function without the efforts of Granville Woods. He invented the troller which provided the contact between the street car and the power wire. This became known as the trolley cars. He invented an electrical railway power system, which today is called the "third rail." He also invented the "induction telegraph system," which allowed train conductors to communicate with each other. Before this invention, there were serious accidents due to fog, darkness, and poor signals.

Edison tried to claim this invention, but lost in court. He also tried to buy his ideas, but Woods unlike Latimer formed his own business. At the time of his death, he had been awarded 150 patents for his scholarship.

Garrett Morgan (1867 - 1963)

The transportation industry is also indebted to Garrett Morgan. Before the invention of the traffic signal, driving was very hazardous. In 1923, he invented the automatic stop sign which regulated traffic. Morgan also noticed the danger experienced by firefighters. They were overcome by fumes and smoke and were not very successful in saving lives. In 1914, he perfected a breathing device, which was called a gas mask. This helped firefighters, chemists, and other people working with dangerous fumes. The military used the mask extensively, beginning in World War I.

George Washington Carver (1864-1943)

The South owes much to George Washington Carver. He introduced the concept of rotating the crops to replenish the soil. The South had produced cotton for years and the soil was becoming infertile. Carver scientifically explained how the soil was being robbed of vital nutrients, and if other crops such as sweet potatoes, soybeans, or peanuts could be grown periodically, it would ultimately increase the cotton yield.

Booker T. Washington also saw the brilliance of this great chemist, and hired him to become a professor at Tuskegee. Carver made over two hundred products from the peanut, and over one hundred from the sweet potato. These products included soap, shampoo, ink, and many shades of dye. From the soybean, Carver extracted flour, cereal, and milk.

Guion Bluford, Jr. (1942 -)

Bluford always enjoyed science. Like Benjamin Banneker, he would take things apart and put them back together. Bluford learned to appreciate science from his father, who was a mechanical engineer. Bluford was a pilot in Vietnam, involved in 144

combat missions, and earned ten medals. He and 34 others were selected from 8,878 to join the space program, called NASA. In 1983, Lt. Colonel Bluford, aboard the 100-ton *Challenger,* became the first African-American to enter space.

Other African-Americans involved with the space program were George Carruthers, who designed the Apollo 16 Far Ultraviolet Camera, which allowed space explorers to record planetary phenomenon. Robert Shurney designed the tires used on the "Moon Buggy Falcon." Bluford along with Isaac Gilliam, Frederick Gregory, and Ronald McNair are four fine African-American astronauts.

Walter Massey (1939 -)

Walter Massey enjoyed math and science as a child. A graduate of Morehouse College, he once said, "I began to see that physics was a way to use mathematics to try to understand the world and that was very exciting." Massey is the first African American to be president of the American Association for the Advancement of Science, the world's largest science organization. He has been a professor in physics and director of Argonne Laboratory. His research lies in measuring the energy of certain liquids and solids. Walter is also Vice President of Research at the University of Chicago.

MORE AFRICAN INVENTORS

Name	Birth	Contribution
James Forten	1766	Method of sewing large heavy sails for big ships

Norbert Rillieux	1806	Sugar refining process
Elijah McCoy	1843	Lubricating cup for machines in operation
Andrew Beard	1849	Jenny coupler, device automatically connecting railroad cars
Daniel Hale Williams	1856	First surgeon to operate on the human heart in America
Frederick Jones	1893	Refrigeration equipment
Percy Julian	1899	Synthesized drug for treatment of glaucoma and rheumatism
Charles Drew	1904	Developed blood plasma and modern blood bank system

Bibliography

Young Adult
The Black Inventors Latimer and Woods.
The Life of Benjamin Banneker, Golden Legacy Magazine. Seattle: Fitzgerald Publishing, 1983.
Haskins, Jim. *The Story of Guion Bluford.* Minneapolis: Carolrhoda Books, 1984.
Winslow, Eugene. *Black Americans in Science and Engineering.* Chicago: Afro-Am Publishing, 1974.

Adult
A Salute to Black Scientists and Inventors. Chicago: Empak Enterprises, 1985.
Carwell, Hattie. *Blacks in Science.* Hicksville: Exposition Press, 1977.

Vocabulary

Write the definition for each word. Write a sentence using each word. Draw a picture of your favorite word on the list or in the chapter.

Almanac
Celestial
Chemistry
Fume
Incubator
Instrument
Mummy
Nutrient
Patent

Phenomena
Physics
Replenish
Research
Smelt
Theory
Transmitter
Yield

Questions

1. Why was it difficult for Africans to maximize their inventions?
2. How did Banneker invent the clock?
3. What was the problem that Matzeliger solved in the shoe industry?
4. What were Woods' inventions?
5. Describe the relationship between Edison and Woods.
6. Who was Lewis Latimer?
7. Why is the South indebted to George Washington Carver?
8. Describe African contributions at NASA.

Exercises

1. Connect science projects to this chapter.
2. Bring in products invented by African-Americans.

Chapter Six

African Culture

What is culture? Do African-Americans have a culture? Culture is more than music, art, language, and food. Culture is everything you believe and do. The foundation of culture is your world view or ethos, which is expressed through your value system, and ultimately in your behavior. The most effective way to control someone's behavior is to determine their value system and ethos. Africans believe in harmony with people, animals, water, land, and air. The African phrase, "Hofu Ni Kwenu," means my concern is for you. Many people in the world value "the survival of the fittest," and look out for number one, rather than being their brother's keeper. Africans did not negate the individual, but felt life would be more enjoyable if each person helped someone else, rather than being self-centered. The individual was taken care of by the group.

VALUES

African	European
We	I
Cooperation	Competition
Internal	External

Nguzo Saba African Value System

UMOJA (Unity)
   To strive for and maintain unity in the family, community, nation, and race.

KUJICHAGULIA (Self-determination)
   To define ourselves, name ourselves, create for ourselves, and speak for ourselves instead of being defined, named, created for, and spoken for by others.

UJIMA (Collective Work and Responsibility)
   To build and maintain our community together and make our sister's and brother's problems our problems, and to solve them together.

UJAMAA (Cooperative Economics)
   To build and maintain our own stores, shops, and other businesses, and to profit from them together.

NIA (Purpose)
   To make our collective vocation the building and developing of our community in order to restore our people to their traditional greatness.

KUUMBA (Creativity)
   To do always as much as we can, in the way we can, in order to leave our community more beautiful and beneficial than we inherited it.

IMANI (Faith)
   To believe with all our heart in our people, our parents, our teachers, our leaders and the righteousness and victory of our struggle.

Africans were the first to believe in one God or monotheism, which started with King Akhenaten. The ethos, world view, or philosophy is best expressed in your relationship to God. The belief in life after death was expressed in Africans building pyramids, temples, and tombs for the "after-life." The process of mummification was a testament of Africans' belief that there was more than a physical life.

The church is a cornerstone of the African-American community, and a major transmitter of culture. There has never, in the history of humans, been a greater form of slavery perpetuated on a people than what was placed on Africans. Africans in slavery prayed to God for a better day, "Bye and Bye." The ability to endure is a strength which religion and music made bearable. People are still wondering how a people so oppressed can still laugh, smile, sing, and believe in a brighter tomorrow.

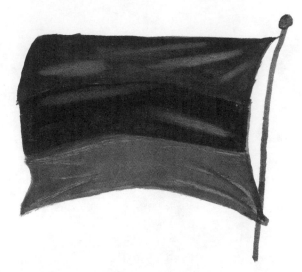

The culture of a people is expressed not only in their value system, but in their flag, pledge, anthem, language, attire, hairstyle, holy days, diet, music, art, and literature.

This is the Liberation Flag created by Marcus Garvey. Red stands for the blood and struggle. Black represents the people and their color. Green stands for land and the future. There can be no future without struggle, and there can be no struggle without people. It is your responsibility to know who you are (Black), know that your purpose is to struggle (Red), and know that your goal is liberation and a better tomorrow (Green). Every flag has meaning and Garvey was careful in selecting yours.

Allegiance of the Flag (U.N.I.A.)

This Flag Is Mine
Here's to this flag of mine the Red, Black, and Green
Hopes in its future bright
Africa has seen
Here's to the Red of it,
Great Nations shall know of it
In time to come.
Red blood shall flow of it.
Great flag of mine.
Here's to the Black of it
Four hundred millions back of it.
Whose destiny depends on it
The Red, Black, and Green of it.
Oh, flag of mine.

Here's to the Green of it
Young men shall dream of it,
Face shot and shells of it,
Maidens shall sing of it
Waving so high
Here's to the whole of it
Colors brought and pole of it
Pleased is my soul with it
Regardless of what is told of it,
Thanks God for giving
Great flag of mine.

"Lift Every Voice and Sing"
James Weldon Johnson

Lift every voice and sing, till earth and heaven ring,
Ring with the harmonies of liberty;
Let our rejoicing rise, high as the listening skies,
Let it resound loud as the rolling sea.
Sing a song full of the faith that the dark past has taught us,
Sing a song full of the hope that the present has brought us;
Facing the rising sun of our new day begun,
Let us march on till victory is won.

Stony the road we trod, bitter the chastening rod,
Felt in the days when hope unborn had died;
Yet with a steady beat, have not our weary feet,
Come to the place for which our fathers signed?

We have come over a way that with tears has been watered,
We have come, treading our path through the blood of the
    slaughtered,
Out from the gloomy past, till now we stand at last,
Where the white gleam of our bright star is cast.

God of our weary years, God of our silent tears,
Thou who hast brought us thus far on the way;
Thou who has by Thy might, led us into the light,
Keep us forever in the path, we pray.

Lest our feet stray from the places, our God, where we met
    Thee,
Lest our hearts, drunk with the wine of the world, we forget
    Thee;
Shadowed beneath Thy hand, may we forever stand,
True to our God, true to our native land.

There were over 1,000 communities in Africa, including Yoruba, Nubian, Ashanti, Masai, and Zulu. These communities and others spoke several languages, which totaled 2,000 different languages. The slave owner did not allow Africans to speak their native language, because he wanted to always know what they were saying. Language is a very strong cultural expression. Other groups such as the Chinese, Japanese, Mexicans, and Puerto Ricans hold onto their language because they recognize its power. There are certain words in one language that do not even exist in another because of differences between value systems. Language is the oral expression of your value system.

In 1974 participants in the Pan-African Conference at Tanzania selected Swahili as the international language for African people. Swahili was already spoken by large numbers of Africans before the decision, and this factor along with its ease in understanding made the decision pragmatic. This does not mean African communities cannot speak other languages, or that African-Americans can't speak English, it simply encourages Africans all over to world to better understand one another by speaking one common language.

Swahili Vocabulary

Phonics
a - short a ah
e - long a
i - long e
o - long o
u - long u oo

Common Words

Jambo	Hello
Habari Gani	What is the news
Njema	Fine
Asante	Thank you
Asante Sana	Thank you very much
Mama	Mother
Baba	Father
Ndada	Sister
Ndugu	Brother
Watoto	Children
Mtoto	Child
Mwalimu	Teacher
Mwanafunzi	Student
Shule	School
Yebo	Yes
La	No
Acha	Stop
Nisamehe	Excuse me
Tafadali	Please
Mzuri	Good
Harambee	Pull together
Pamoja Tutashinda	Together we will win
Mzee	Elder
Chakula	Food
Choo	Toilet
Hodi hodi	Hurry
Tutaonana	Good-bye

Numbers

Moja	One
Mbili	Two
Tatu	Three
Nne	Four
Tano	Five
Sita	Six
Saba	Seven
Nane	Eight
Tisa	Nine
Kumi	Ten

There are almost five billion people in the world. Nine of every ten people possess color: yellow, black, brown, or red. Asians lead the world in population with one billion living in China alone. Africans are the second largest group with 700 million. Africans live all over the world, with the largest numbers in the African triangle, Africa (500 million), Caribbean islands and South America (160 million), and the United States (40 million). Africans are not the minority, unless we do not see we're related to our brothers and sisters in the triangle.

Africans have always worn bright colors. This cultural expression illustrates the desire to bring vitality to everyday living. Males can be found wearing short or long dashikis. The short dashiki is worn for regular occasions, and the long is displayed for special events. Females often wear a head wrap, called a gele (gala). The female top is called a buba, and the bottom is a loppa.

The materials for dashikis, geles, bubas, and loppas can come from a wide range of sources. Africans living in tropical climates would choose a lighter fabric than those living in arctic regions. One of the royal fabrics is called Kinte (kenta) cloth, from Ghana.

God gave everyone good hair. People who live near the equator need short hair, so the scalp can breathe. People living in cold climates need long hair, to keep them warm. Natural hair is easy to manage, inexpensive to maintain, and allows participation in various activities. Unfortunately, some African-Americans don't swim because they do not want their hair to return to its natural state.

In the 1960's the natural haircut was a political statement expressing Black pride. Many hair care companies and wig manufacturers made it a hairstyle and altered the length and color. Consequently it became a fad that eventually drifted away. Many girls still wonder why their mothers put a hot comb to their hair, which often burns. With the recent movement of uni-sexualization many males are also trying to look feminine and European.

Cornrowing is an ancient hairstyle handed down from Queen Nefertiti to today. It is representative of the symmetry and order of African women's beauty and an expression of communication with the universe. Traditionally among the Yoruba, the most decorative and intricate styles were worn by queens. Not only was cornrowing a symbol of status during those times, but was also a sign of maturity.

Young girls and older women wore simple basic styles, while marriageable women wore the more elaborate versions.

Every race or group has holy days. There is a difference between holy days and holidays. The latter are days celebrating other people or events that are not necessarily germane to your race or group. Most people use holidays to rest and have a good

time. A holy day should not only give you a good time, but also provide historical appreciation and inspiration for the future.

Some African-American holy days are:

January 15	Dr. Martin Luther King's Birthday
February	Black Liberation Month (Founded by Carter G. Woodson in honor of Frederick Douglass' birthday)
May 19	Malcolm X's Birthday
August 17	Marcus Garvey's Birthday
December 26 - Jan. 1	Kwanzaa (Founded by Maulana Karenga in 1966 as a non-religious, non-hero holy season. Kwanzaa, which means First Fruits or the harvest, is an opportunity for Africans to celebrate the fruits of their labor over the year.)

The food for holy day parties can include mango, avocado, plantain, watermelon, millet, okra, blackeye peas, yams, seafood, and chicken curry.

Africans' ability to survive has been based on a strong commitment to God and the gift of music. It was the African drum that kept the African community informed. It was singing on the plantation that made the work tolerable and the time move faster. Africans have shared this gift with the world.

We have excelled in gospel, jazz, blues, classical, reggae, rhythm and blues, and pop music. The artists W.C. Handy, Billie Holiday, Duke Ellington, Leontyne Price, Aretha Franklin, Stevie Wonder, Wynton Marsalis, Bob Marley, and Gil Scott Heron are all outstanding examples. Many contemporary artists, who do not understand the history and power of music in the African experience, are producing records for exploitation rather than liberation. Songs that are vulgar, sexually suggestive, and immoral are inconsistent with the African drum. Gil Scott Heron and Stevie Wonder are fine examples of musicians who feel "entertainment" should lead to "inner attainment."

African people were the first to write using hieroglyphics, and the first to use paper or papyrus. The African-American contribution in literature began with Phillis Wheatley and Paul Laur-

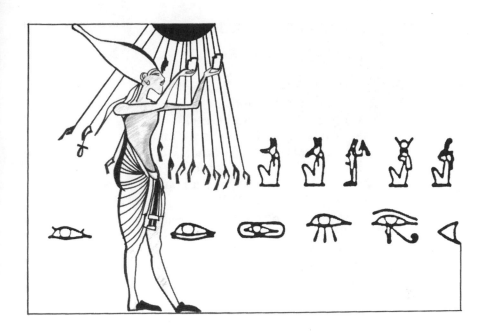

ence Dunbar. This fine tradition continued with the Harlem Renaissance of the 1920's, with writers such as Langston Hughes, Claude McKay, and James Weldon Johnson. The 1930's - 1940's provided the brilliance of Richard Wright and Zora Neale Hurston. The 1950's -1970's and particularly the second renaissance of the 1960's, brought Gwendolyn Brooks, James Baldwin, Leroi Jones, Sonia Sanchez, and Haki Madhubuti. Ayi Kwei Armah and Chinua Achebe continue this rich African literary tradition.

Three excellent poems that tell the African story were written by Langston Hughes, Lerone Bennett, Jr. and Margaret Burroughs. They are offered for your review.

Harlem
by Langston Hughes
What happens to a dream deferred:
Does it dry up like a raisin in the sun?
Or fester like a sore
And then run?
Does it stink like rotten meat?
Or crust and sugar over like a syrupy sweet?
Maybe it just sags like a heavy load.
Or does it explode?

Booker T. and W.E.B. DuBois

by Dudley Randall

"It seems to me," said Booker T.,
"It shows a mighty lot of cheek
To study chemistry and Greek
When Mister Charlie needs a hand
To hoe the cotton on his land,
And when Miss Ann looks for a cook,
Why stick your nose inside a book?"

"I don't agree," said W.E.B.,
"If I should have the drive to seek
Knowledge of chemistry or Greek,
I'll do it. Charles and Miss can look
Another place for hand or cook.
Some men rejoice in skill of hand,
And some in cultivating land,
But there are others who maintain
The right to cultivate the brain."

"It seems to me," said Booker T.,
"That all you folks have missed the boat
Who shout about the right to vote,
And spend vain days and sleepless nights
In uproar over civil rights.
Just keep your mouths shut, do not grouse,
But work, and save, and buy a house."

"I don't agree," said W.E.B.,
"For what can property avail
If dignity and justice fail?
Unless you help to make the laws,
They'll steal your house with trumped-up clause.
A rope's as tight, a fire as hot,
No matter how much cash you've got,
Speak soft, and try your little plan,
But as for me, I'll be a man."

"It seems to me," said Booker T.
"I don't agree,"
Said W.E.B.

What Should I Tell My Children Who Are Black
by Margaret Burroughs
What shall I tell my children who are black
Of what it means to be a captive in this dark skin?
What shall I tell my dear one, fruit of my womb,
Of how beautiful they are when everywhere they turn
They are faced with the abhorrence of everything that is black.
The night is black and so is the boogyman.
Villains are black with black hearts.
A black cow gives no milk.
A black hen lays no eggs.
Bad news comes bordered in black, mourning clothes black,
Storm clouds, black and devil's food is black...

What shall I tell my dear ones raised in a white world
A place where white has been made to represent
All that is good and pure and fine and decent,
Where clouds are white and dolls, and heaven
Surely is a white, white place with angels
Robed in white, and cotton candy and ice cream
And milk and ruffled Sunday dresses

And dream houses and long sleek Cadillacs
And angel's food is white...all, all...white.

What can I say therefore, when my child comes home
In tears because a playmate has called him black, big-lipped, flat-nosed
And nappy headed? What will he think when I dry
his tears and whisper, "Yes, that's true but no
Less beautiful and dear."

How shall I lift up his head, get him to square
His shoulders, look his adversaries in the eye,
Confident in the knowledge of his worth, serene
Under his sable skin and proud of his own beauty.

What can I do to give him strength that he may
Come through life's adversities as a whole human
Being unwrapped and human in a world of biased
Laws and inhuman practices, that he might

Survive. And survive he must! For who knows?
Perhaps this black child here bears the genius
To discover the cure for...cancer or to chart
The course for exploration of the universe.
So, he must survive for the good of all humanity.
He must and will survive.

I have drunk deeply of late from the fountain of
My black culture, sat at the knee and learned
From Mother Africa, discovered the truth of my heritage,
The truth, so often obscured and omitted
And I find I have much to say to my black children.

I will lift up their heads in proud blackness
With the story of their fathers and their fathers' fathers.
And I shall take them into a way back time of
Kings and Queens who ruled the Nile, and measured the stars
and discovered the law of mathematics.
Upon whose backs have been built the wealth of two continents.

I will tell him this and more,
and his heritage shall be his weapon and his armor;
will make him strong enough to win any battle he may face.

And since this story is often obscured,
I must sacrifice to find it for my children,
even as I sacrifice to feed, cloth, and shelter them.
So this I will do for them if I love them
None will do it for me. I must find the truth of heritage for
myself and pass it on to them.
In years to come I believe because
I have armed them with the truth, My children and
Their children's children will venerate me.
For it's the truth that will make us free!

Bibliography

Adults

Bell, Roseann, edited. *Sturdy Black Bridges*. New York: Anchor Press, 1979.

Chapman, Abraham, edited. *Black Voices*. New York: New American Library, 1968.

Jones, Nathan. *Sharing The Old, Old Story*. Winona: St. Mary's Press, 1982.

Karenga, Maulana. *Kwanzaa*. Los Angeles: Kawaida Publications, 1977.

Vocabulary

Write a definition for each word. Write a sentence using each word. Draw a picture of your favorite word on the list or in the chapter.

Arctic	Monotheism
Elaborate	Philosophy
Ethos	Status
Exploit	Symmetry
Fad	Tropical
Germane	Vulgar

Questions

1. What is African culture?
2. What are the different ways that culture is expressed?
3. What is the meaning of the Liberation Flag?
4. Describe the African triangle and its numbers.
5. In honor of an African-American holy day, how would you dress and eat?
6. What is your criteria for beauty? Include skin and eye color and hair texture.
7. Give the dates for Malcolm X and Marcus Garvey's birthdays.

Exercises

1. Trace African music from Africa, to slavery, and to the present, and include reggae.
2. Listen to Gil Scott Heron's "Angel Dust" and "B Movie," Stevie Wonder's "Happy Birthday," and "Ebony-Ivory," Run DMC's "Black History Rap," and Gary Byrd's "You Wear the Crown."
3. Plan a feast and wear African dress.
4. Read some of the writings from the authors mentioned in this chapter.

Chapter Seven

Lessons from History

History should be more than remembering names, dates and events. It should do more than keep you in the past. We should learn lessons or concepts from history; mistakes should be avoided, and strengths reinforced and utilized in the present and future.

What do the pyramids mean to us today? Does Imhotep have an impact on our present lives? What is the relative significance that Greeks studied in Egypt? Why should we not forget the invaders along the coast and the horrors of the Middle Passage? Where is the relevance of David Walker and Nat Turner? What are the messages we can learn from Delany, Douglass, Washington, DuBois, Garvey, Malcolm, King, Farrakhan, and Jackson? Does Toussaint L'Ouverture have an impact on our lives? Would the African-American economy be stronger if our scientists had been able to produce their inventions? What does culture have to do with you and me?

The psychology of becoming free is contingent upon understanding the slave making process. Before Africans went to slave owners, they were "seasoned" by slave makers. These men were charged with the responsibility of achieving four goals to make a good slave.

1. Place fear in slaves by beating them or killing one publicly as a example.
2. Teach them to be loyal and identify with the owner, by giving any traitors favors for informing.
3. Teach them to feel inferior by always showing Whites in positions of power.
4. Teach them to hate Africa and anything Black, by harsh words and giving special favors to light-skinned Africans.

The psychology of becoming free requires the reverse of the slave making process.

Fear

Queen N' Zinga, Harriet Tubman, Malcom X, Martin Luther King, Jr. and many others were great because they were not afraid of death.

Lesson: If you are not prepared to die for something you are not fit to live for anything.

Loyalty

There have been at least 265 documented slave revolts. They were successful because they illustrated resistance and kept the system of slavery unstable, but most of them were thwarted because traitors within the race told the owners. Toussaint L'Ouverture had beaten Napoleon in battle but trusted him in the negotiation, and was imprisoned.

Loyalty and trust have been historical problems with Africans, originating when they allowed invaders to settle along the coast under the disguise of peaceful traders. Africans historically treat other people from the viewpoint of their own value system, rather than understanding the other person's values and acting accordingly.

Lesson: Look for the good in everyone, but never turn your back. Never trust people outside your race and be careful of those within. There are three criteria of Blackness: color, consciousness, and culture. To be Black or African means to look Black, think Black, and act Black.

Inferior

Chattel slavery required chains, slave makers, owners, and overseers. Slavery was always in jeopardy as long as slaves actually saw its physical evidence. Mental slavery requires the control of the mind, by teaching the enslaved person to feel inferior. This form of slavery does not require chains, slave makers, owners, and overseers; you simply need words and images from teachers, books, and television that make a person feel inferior. Eventually, you will need less of the above, because the victims will convince new generations of the same.

"His - story" means people often tell their story rather than the truth. White history makes Greece the origin of civilization, but Herodotus is not the father of history and Hippocrates is not the father of medicine. Many Africans believe White owned businesses are better than their own.

Lesson: Be proud of your history, remember your ancestors built the first civilization. Africans were the first to write, compute, build great buildings, and believe in one God. Because your ancestors were great, you can be also — support Black owned businesses, and consider starting one yourself.

100

Color

People who are secure are comfortable with differences; only insecure people need to rationalize superiority, because of differences. Insecure people have made color or the lack of it a standard of beauty. When Europeans raped African women and babies were conceived, the offspring were primarily light-skinned. The owners were partial toward the mulattoes. This created jealousy between light-skinned children, who mostly worked in the house, and dark-skinned children who usually worked in the field.

Africans noticed the obvious favoritism and many today do not like their blackness, believe good hair is long and straight, and pretty eyes are blue or green. Many Black colleges used to require that a picture be submitted with the application to eliminate dark-skinned students. Mothers were often found telling their children, "don't bring home no dark-skinned spouse." Some African-Americans still believe marrying light or White will produce pretty babies.

Lesson: If having color is negative, why do Whites risk skin cancer trying to get a sun tan? The more color or melanin a

person has, the more the aging process will be delayed and the skin kept smooth. Larger amounts of melanin allow more sun to be absorbed, which is necessary for vitamin D in the production of brain cells. Good hair is natural hair that is clean, inexpensive, easy to manage, allows the scalp to breathe, prevents lice, and permits a person to sweat and swim easily.

Mistake

Human beings are the most intelligent animals on the planet. Their advanced brains can either be used for constructive or destructive purposes. God gave humans the world and the fullness thereof, which includes the land, air, and water. Humans can either work in harmony with nature and themselves or against themselves.

Africans used much of their intellect to build pyramids, temples, tombs, and universities. Europeans used most of their brains to develop military weapons. This is best expressed today, where the United States is involved in a nuclear arms race to see how many more times they can blow the world up over Russia. The government allocates fifty cents of every dollar to defense, and two cents to education.

Lesson: If you value what you have, be prepared to defend it. The building of the pyramids was not enough, if there has not also been a self-defense system developed.

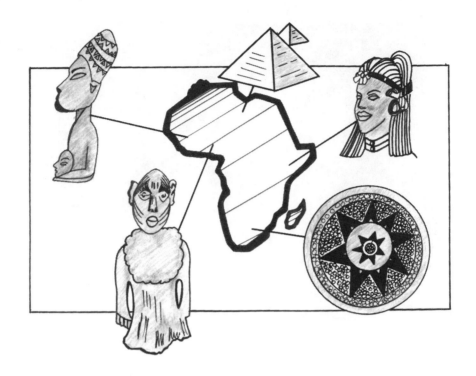

Mistake

When Asians, Arabs, and Europeans came to Africa, they saw a lack of unity. Africans were divided into 1000 communities speaking 2,000 languages. When the numbers are in a people's favor, most people and especially Africans don't feel the need for unity.

The real minorities are not Africans but Europeans, who represent about ten percent of the world's population, but desire to control over sixty percent of its resources. The absence of color and the shortage of numbers, has given them a paranoia often called racism, and a strong sense of unity. Africans on the other hand, with large amounts of melanin and sizable numbers, did not see a need for unity. Even today, in African-American communities where everyone is Black, people seldom speak to each other; but when Africans become the minority in the suburbs, they welcome the opportunity to speak to another African person.

Lesson: One hundred unified Europeans can defeat 500 Africans divided into ten groups. Racial unity is more important than community or individual differences.

Mistake

Africans placed great trust in their leaders. When Arabs and Europeans invaded, they saw kings had great power. In America, Africans placed great trust in Douglass, Washington, Garvey, Muhammad, Malcolm, and King, but when these men died, the movement slowed down. The leaders were mostly men and primarily from the church.

Lesson: Leaders should come from all groups, not just the church and women should be included. We should separate the *message* from the *messenger*, because the latter dies, but the message continues. The message for liberation includes owning businesses, land, and schools, and believing in self-defense, boycotts, marches, non-violence, and equal opportunity.

Mistake

African-Americans have given much to American industry. They invented many items including the shoe lasting machine, telephone transmitter, third rail, carbon filaments, clock, lawn mower, stove, refrigerator, lubricator, soap, ink, and shampoo. It was difficult for Banneker, Matzeliger, Morgan, Latimer, Carver, Woods, and others to secure and protect their patents. Many Africans did not have the faith or capital to start their own businesses.

The African community should be rich with the ingenuity of these inventions. Unfortunately, Matzeliger died before he could capitalize off the shoe industry; Latimer gave all his skills to Edison rather than starting his own enterprise. Granville Woods was a shining example of an African-American scientist who remained independent, but never really had the capital to maximize his telephone transmitter, telegraphony, trolley, third rail, egg incubator, and induction telegraph.

The obstacles for African-American business development lay in attitude, capital, and racial solidarity. The African community spends over ninety percent of their income with other people. Many African-American professionals still desire working for the Fortune 500 rather than starting their own corporations. Arabs, Koreans, and other immigrants, with little education but strong business skills, grow rich off the African community. The problem of capital can be resolved when the attitude of "do for self" and racial unity become a reality. Marcus Garvey and Elijah Muhammad provided fine examples of those who encouraged economic development. W.E.B. DuBois pointed out that Garvey lacked sound business principles, therefore people with guts like Garvey and Muhammad need assistance from DuBois's "talented tenth," to revitalize the African community.

Lesson: Africans must make economics as much a priority as religion, politics, and education. The African-American community has many churches, politicians, and educators, but very few employers.

Strengths

Some African-Americans believe they are only good in music and sports, but Africans are multi-talented. They have done well in whatever they were given an opportunity. Benjamin Banneker just wanted a chance to write an almanac, design Washington, and make a clock. The Tuskegee Airmen just wanted an assignment to fly. Jackie Robinson just wanted the position to hit, run, and field.

Lesson: Africans are good in math and music, sports and science, but greatness depends on hard work and opportunity.

Strength

Africans' love for education began at the Grand Lodge of Wa'at in Egypt. African-Americans risked death during slavery trying to read under a candle or moonlight. After slavery, many Africans created independent Black schools. Mary McLeod Bethune founded Bethune-Cookman. The Black colleges continue to receive the fewest number of Black students, but produce the largest number of graduates.

The Clara Muhammad schools started under the leadership of Elijah Muhammad and their graduates are fine examples of Black excellence. The Council of Independent Black Schools (CIBI) combine academic and cultural awareness in students to build the Black nation.

Lesson: Always value education. No one can control a person who knows his or her identity, purpose, and direction. We are an African people, whose purpose is the liberation of our race through the Nguzo Saba African Value System.

Strength

Africans have always valued family. The African proverb, "children are the reward of life," saved them.

It was faith that made the Middle Passage endurable. It was faith that made working from sunrise to sunset go faster. It was faith that made the Depression of the 1930's just another decade. Africans commit suicide less often than anyone else, and yet earn less income. White men, who earn more than anyone, lead the country in suicide.

It was faith that helped Africans avoid hating their enemies. It was ministers based on faith and in the church, that led those 265 slave revolts. It was the church that founded and supported Black colleges. It was the church that Jesse Jackson and other politicians used to launch their campaigns.

Lesson: African-Americans must use their faith and the church beyond survival to growth and liberation. The church must be open seven days a week providing day care, food co-ops, tutorial and rites of passage programs, credit unions, housing developments, employment training, and more jobs.

Strength

Africans are very brave people. Hannibal, N'Zinga, and L'Ouverture fought the Romans, Portuguese, and French with smaller numbers and won. African-Americans have fought in every American war, with Crispus Attucks being the first to die, in our quest to be free. This bravery is shown while the KKK, in large numbers along with gangs wearing specially designed jackets and caps, beat smaller numbers of men, women, and children.

Bravery is not always shown on the front line, but in the courtroom. Muhammad Ali, the greatest heavyweight champion refused to fight for what he did not believe. The next war could take place in Africa or in the Caribbean.

Lesson: Before you fight a war for other people and their exploitation of other nations, fight for freedom for your own people and the removal of race as a tool of economic exploitation.

109

Strength

There have always been a few Africans whose spirits were never broken. They never forgot Africa and the beauty of being Black. They led slave revolts, opened schools, wrote books, and gave speeches. They refused to move to the back of the bus. They marched, boycotted, and sat at lunch counters. They started businesses, celebrated African holy days, and displayed the red, black, and green flag.

Lesson: The future of the race depends not on DuBois's talented tenth, but on the committed few who will carry the torch.

Will you carry the torch for justice, freedom, and liberation?

I hope this book has helped you gain knowledge of your history, and has made you proud.

I hope it will inspire you to academic achievement that would have made Imhotep proud.

I hope that you will become disciplined, serious, and feel a responsibility to contribute to your race.

Your brother,
Jawanza Kunjufu

Bibliography

Adult

Karenga, Maulana. *Introduction to Black Studies.* Los Angeles: Kawaida Publications, 1982.

Stampp, Kenneth. *The Peculiar Institution.* New York: Vintage, 1956.

Vocabulary

Write the definition for each word. Write a sentence using each word. Draw a picture of your favorite word on the list or in the chapter.

Chattel	Perpetuate
Concepts	Portray
Consciousness	Priority
Culprit	Process
Document	Psychology
Melanin	Resolve
Negotiate	Solidarity
Partial	Technical
	Thwart

Questions

1. Why should we learn history?
2. What were the four objectives of the slave maker?
3. List the liberation messages.
4. Why is the message more important than the messenger?
5. What is the nuclear arms buildup?
6. Who is the world minority?
7. Why was Granville Woods a shining example?
8. Why are African-Americans involved more in music and sports than in math and science?
9. What are the strengths of African families?
10. What saved Africans?
11. List the African mistakes and strengths.
12. Will you carry the torch? Explain.

Exercises

1. Write a play and include some African mistakes and strengths.

2. Play Dr. King's and Malcom X's records and tapes and talk about fear.
3. Let the students select their favorite message and attempt to convince the class of its viability.

Index

114